W9-AGO-805

Praise for
THE **GAP** AND THE **GAIN**

"There's a science to achievement, but an art to fulfillment; and achievement without fulfillment is the ultimate failure. The GAP and the GAIN is a powerful concept that empowers the reader to have access to fulfillment throughout their journey of achievement. This energy of fulfillment is medicine for the mind, body, and soul."

— **Kien Vuu MD**, The Performance and Longevity Doctor, best-selling author of *Thrive State*, and assistant professor of Medicine, UCLA

"When I first learned about the GAP from Dan years ago, I realized that not only was I living in the GAP but I had pulled my whole team into it with me! Being in the GAIN is inspiring and powerful. It helps me appreciate where I'm at and helps me create the growth I truly want."

— **JJ Virgin**, *New York Times* best-selling author and Inc. 5000 founder

"Here is the book that would have saved me a decade of misery had I read it before blindly pursuing what I thought was success. Thank you, Dan, and Ben, for telling the truth that nobody wants to acknowledge—that goals in and of themselves won't make us happy. There's a lot in this book for anyone who wants to not just achieve but actually live."

— **Jeff Goins**, best-selling author of *The Art of Work*

"If you're struggling in any area of your life and want to truly succeed, you must learn how to live your life in the GAIN and stay out of the GAP. Personally, I've overcome many struggles in my life—from nearly dying in a head-on car accident to almost dying of cancer to overcoming severe depression—and I did it by living my life in the GAIN and staying out of the GAP. Even in the darkest moments. Read this book—it will show you how to overcome anything life sends your way and find happiness here and now."

— **Hal Elrod**, author of *The Miracle Morning* series and *The Miracle Equation*

"I've spent my life studying what it takes to be THE BEST in the world at what you do. This book shows you how to become your best in a way that also makes you happy, rather than the approaches most people attempt that make them miserable."

— **Bo Eason**, former NFL safety, author of *There's No Plan B for Your A-Game*

"The Gap and The Gain *is another indispensable book, and concept, from Dan Sullivan. There isn't a day that goes by that his wisdom doesn't guide my company. This book is another gem."*

— **Chris Voss**, author of *Never Split the Difference*

"This book will challenge everything you think you know about achievement. Ben and Dan show you how to get out of the GAP and into the GAIN, making you and your teams not only successful, but also happy. Prepare to be dazzled!"

— **Alinka Rutkowska**, *USA Today* and *Wall Street Journal* best-selling author, CEO of Leaders Press

"Two minutes into this book, I realized it was going to change my life. The clear writing and chewy ideas speed you along—you won't want to put it down until it's finished. The Gap and The Gain *is a master class that you can immediately integrate into your work and life to make both even better."*

— **Shane Snow**, author of *Dream Teams*

"All three of Dr. Benjamin Hardy's books are powerful, unique, and highly practical. Dan Sullivan's teachings have tangibly upgraded my life and business. Their new book, The Gap and The Gain, *is essential reading for any leader or high achiever who wants both more happiness and to reach their highest level of performance."*

— **Michael Hyatt**, *New York Times* best-selling author

"No one knows entrepreneurs like Dan Sullivan, the world's most successful coach of entrepreneurs. He and his co-author, Benjamin Hardy, have written a book for those entrepreneurs who are disappointed, frustrated, or fearful they are falling short. And most exciting of all, the book, The Gap and The Gain, *has an instant solution to their anxieties."*

— **Richard A. Viguerie**, chairman of American Target Advertising, Inc.

"The concepts in this book have made me so much happier in my building my companies and in my life journey, and those around me have benefited because of that."

— **Cameron Herold**, founder of COO Alliance, host of the *Second in Command* podcast, and author of *Vivid Vision*

"Understanding the GAP and the GAIN is the single most important concept for any entrepreneur. Reading this book and implementing its ideas will become immediately transformative for visionary leaders in life and in business."

— **Justin Breen**, founder of BrEpic Communications, Strategic Coach 10x Ambition Client

"If there is one concept that can shift the way you operate your business, this is it. Don't miss it. It's so simple you can start implementing it today, yet so profound, it'll impact the way you operate forever."

— **Nick Nanton**, Esq., EMMY® Award-winning director and producer, *Wall Street Journal* best-selling author, and Global Shield Humanitarian Award recipient

"Don't worry. Be happy. Easy to say. Tough to do, especially for entrepreneurs, hard-wired for never-ending achievement. Dan and Ben's book demystifies the process of achieving happiness, one of our most essential human desires."

— **Kary Oberbrunner**, CEO of Igniting Souls and *Wall Street Journal* and *USA Today* best-selling author of *Unhackable*

"I've collaborated with both Dan and Ben in the past. In a world saturated with attention-obsessed wannabe influencer knuckleheads, they are those rarest of breeds—smart fellows with something genuinely new and interesting to say."

— **Hugh MacLeod**, author of *Ignore Everybody* and co-founder of Gapingvoid

"Most entrepreneurs aren't happy. Being your own boss was supposed to "fix" everything, but it didn't and you're more stressed-out than ever. The Gap and The Gain *gives you the tools and mindset to continually grow in both your success and happiness."*

— **Evan Carmichael**, author of *Built to Serve*

"Staying focused on the ideal and living in the GAP is exhausting. And it can suck the creativity out of you! Staying out of the GAP helps me to continue to move toward who I believe I am capable of becoming. I am more present, more grateful, and a happier human."

— **Mary Lucas Atwood**, president and CEO, Advisor Consulting Hub

"Learning about the GAP and teaching myself to live in the GAIN has been the fuel to inspire me to grow and to show my team how to measure success every day. Knowing this process empowers me to help others with it daily."

— **Don Cooper**, founder of Innovator Industrial, host of *The Amplifier Podcast*, Strategic Coach 10X Ambition Client

"The concept of the GAP and the GAIN is a monumental mindshift that is critical for any entrepreneur, athlete, leader, parent, or anyone wanting a relationship to last. I know this seems like it's for everyone but that's because it is...it changes how you will perceive your achievements and those of others...happiness is possible after all."

— **Lisa M Cini**, founder and CEO, Mosaic Design Studio, Infinite Living & BestLivingTech.com and best-selling author

"This book is a must read for all entrepreneurs. The GAP and the GAIN *is such a simple but complex concept. This book has given me the awareness that I not only spend way too much time in the GAP, but also that I'm not alone in feeling this way."*

— **Nick Sonnenberg**, Founder/CEO of www.getleverage.com, Author and Podcaster.

"The GAP and the GAIN *is one of the most important tools you can use for experiencing greater happiness, confidence, and success. For over two decades, thanks to Dan Sullivan, Babs Smith, and Strategic Coach, I've had the opportunity of experiencing the benefits of training my brain to measure my progress correctly—and it has led to greater freedom and resilience. Now, thanks to the incredible writer Ben Hardy helping Dan to codify this process, this book will help you to transform every experience you, your team, and your family have into a gain. Buy this book and read it!"*

— **Joe Polish**, founder of Genius Network

"In the gold exploration business, it can be a long time between discoveries and a long time from discovery to mine. Regularly reminding ourselves of our "wins" and just how far we have come provides the positive mindset our team needs to propel us to the next discovery."

— **Ingrid Hibbard**, LL.B, president and CEO, Pelangio Exploration

THE
GAP
AND THE
GAIN

ALSO BY DAN SULLIVAN AND DR. BENJAMIN HARDY

Books

*Who Not How: The Formula to Achieve Bigger Goals through Accelerating Teamwork**

ALSO BY DR. BENJAMIN HARDY

Personality Isn't Permanent: Break Free from Self-Limiting Beliefs and Rewrite Your Story

Willpower Doesn't Work: Discover the Hidden Keys to Success

*Available from Hay House
Please visit:

Hay House USA: www.hayhouse.com®
Hay House Australia: www.hayhouse.com.au
Hay House UK: www.hayhouse.co.uk
Hay House India: www.hayhouse.co.in

THE GAP AND THE GAIN

THE HIGH ACHIEVERS' GUIDE TO HAPPINESS, CONFIDENCE, AND SUCCESS

DAN SULLIVAN
FOUNDER OF **STRATEGIC COACH**

WITH **DR. BENJAMIN HARDY**

HAY HOUSE, INC.
Carlsbad, California • New York City
London • Sydney • New Delhi

Published in the United States by: Hay House, Inc.: www.hayhouse.com® ***Published in Australia by:*** Hay House Australia Pty. Ltd.: www.hayhouse.com.au • ***Published in the United Kingdom by:*** Hay House UK, Ltd.: www.hayhouse.co.uk • ***Published in India by:*** Hay House Publishers India: www.hayhouse.co.in

Project editor: Melody Guy • *Indexer:* Joan Shapiro
Cover design: Jason Gabbert • *Interior design:* Nick C. Welch
Illustration: Property of The Strategic Coach Inc.

Cataloging-in-Publication Data is on file at the Library of Congress

Hardcover ISBN: 978-1-4019-6436-8
E-book ISBN: 978-1-4019-6437-5
Audiobook ISBN: 978-1-4019-6500-6

10 9 8 7 6 5 4 3 2 1
1st edition, October 2021

Printed in the United States of America

Dan Sullivan's Dedication

The "GAP and GAIN" achievements, since 1995, of more than 20,000 ambitious, talented, and successful entrepreneurs enabled us to write this book. The reports and accounts you'll read represent 60,000+ years of collective entrepreneurial transformation.

These admirable men and women provided us with ***overwhelming proof that measuring progress backward quickly and easily becomes a fundamentally positive and permanent human skill.***

The GAP and The GAIN is proving uniquely useful for visionary high achievers in every entrepreneurial field.

This is especially true for innovative high achievers who, until learning the GAP and the GAIN distinction, seldom felt happy with their remarkable results, and never for very long.

Entrepreneurs' growing mastery of this single concept dramatically changes their lives in much happier directions. By simply measuring each day backward, and not against their endless ideals, they increase their individual confidence and organizational capability on a daily basis.

Their individual lives, and the lives of those they serve, work with, and live with, improve in every area of commitment and purpose.

My collaborator, Dr. Ben Hardy, explained to me that from the perspective of psychological research, our findings in this book are probably the most extensive and comprehensive to be continually and exclusively derived from outlier *individuals.*

In other words, these thousands of entrepreneurs are not normal people and they don't live normal lives. They were born as lifetime goal setters and overachievers. No one had to teach them how to be successful. To a person, they are self-motivated, self-managing, and self-measuring.

Their single fundamental problem is simple to state: throughout their successful journey since childhood of always achieving bigger and better, they missed the classes on being happy.

That goes for me too. My single greatest stroke of good fortune in my life was meeting and marrying my lifetime business partner, Babs Smith. Since 1982, her wisdom and teamwork have kept me on a marvelously productive success path, which has also provided great enjoyment for both of us, and thousands of others.

Benjamin Hardy's Dedication

To Lauren, for being the most important GAIN in my life. Thank you for your love and support. Thank you for helping me become better. Thank you for appreciating my GAINS while helping me see how much further we can go.

To Kaleb, Jordan, and Logan, for each of your incredible GAINS over the past several years. It's inspiring to see much how much you each learn and grow each day. You also help me to become better every day as well. We're all growing together. Thanks for staying in the GAIN with me when I make mistakes.

To my parents, Philip Hardy and Susan Knight, for the GAINS you both have made in your lives, and for the GAINS you've helped me make in mine. Thank you for loving me and investing so much into me. Thank you for always seeing me and my life in the GAIN.

To Tucker Max, for all the GAINS you've helped me make both personally and professionally. Thank you for editing my books. But also, for helping me think much more clearly as a writer and as a person. Also, thank you for all the deep conversations you've had with me, helping me through emotional issues or getting unstuck. You've helped me make very meaningful and important GAINS, for which I'll always be grateful.

Finally, to Joe Polish, for creating Genius Network and introducing me to Dan and Babs. I've created incredible GAINS as a person and entrepreneur because of your enthusiasm, ideas, and the connection network you've created. Thank you very much, Joe!

CONTENTS

"The way to measure your progress is backward against where you started, not against your ideal."

—Dan Sullivan

INTRODUCTION

Why Most People Aren't Happy

"There is no way to happiness—happiness is the way."

—THICH NHAT HANH

Thomas Jefferson penned the *Declaration of Independence* in 1776, and Americans have been unhappy ever since.

One specific phrase has come to define American culture and psychology: "Life, Liberty and ***the pursuit*** of Happiness."

Even as a young man, Jefferson struggled with the idea of happiness. He believed we should aspire to it, but that its actual attainment was likely impossible.

In 1763, the 20-year-old Jefferson wrote a letter to a college classmate, John Page. He shared a recent experience of being rejected by a woman.

> "Perfect happiness, I believe, was never intended by the Deity to be the lot of one of his creatures in this world; but that he has very much put in our power the nearness of our approaches to it, is what I have steadfastly believed."[1]

The *pursuit* of an unreachable happiness was part of Jefferson's credo.

This philosophy was the basis of his thinking not only as a romantically inclined youth, but also as a middle-aged man who was envisioning the principles of a new nation.

What Jefferson didn't realize is, with that single statement in the *Declaration of Independence*, he framed the experience of "Happiness" as *unattainable*. That notion would go on to shape the culture of America.

By saying happiness is something we're *pursuing*, the direct implication is that *we don't have it now.*

You don't pursue something you already have.

Even if we've already achieved something great, this pursuing keeps happiness always up ahead and around the corner.

Happiness is after the *next* achievement.

Happiness is somewhere in the distant future.

Happiness is *out there.*

But happiness is never *here.*

If you think this is a stretch, a recent poll found that *only 14 percent* of American adults say they're very happy.[2]

I'm not blaming all American unhappiness on one of America's most important founding fathers. But ideas can create culture, and culture is perhaps the most powerful force shaping human identity and decision-making.[3]

The consequences of this framing aren't small. By embracing the pursuit of happiness, we rob ourselves of happiness in the here and now. We fail to appreciate who we are and what we've done to this point.

When your happiness is tied to something in the future, then your present is diminished. You don't feel happy, confident, or successful. But maybe in the future you will be, or so the logic goes.

MAKING HAPPINESS A BURDEN

"It's an enormous burden to be in the mindset that happiness is something you need to go out and get."

When you're chasing happiness externally, it's because you're disconnected internally. And when you're disconnected internally, then you're trying to fill a GAP.

Are you in the GAP?

In the early '90s, Dan Sullivan, the world's foremost entrepreneurial coach, discovered how pervasive the GAP was among his highly successful clients, as well as people generally.

He exposed the GAP as a toxic mindset that stopped people from being happy and appreciating their lives. He knew that until people got out of the GAP, they'd never be as happy or successful as they could be.

He set out to help people get out of the GAP.

The GAP and The GAIN became one of Dan's most crucial and transformational concepts. Until now, this concept has been hidden behind the exclusive walls of Dan Sullivan's Strategic Coach program.

THE GAP AND THE GAIN

> *"Your future growth and progress are now based in your understanding about the difference between the two ways in which you can measure yourself: against an ideal, which puts you in what I call 'the GAP,' and against your starting point, which puts you in 'the GAIN,' appreciating all that you've accomplished."*
>
> —DAN SULLIVAN

The GAP is found in both mundane and monumental experiences. You could be in the GAP about getting the smaller half of a cookie (more on this later). Or you could be in the GAP about your entire past—wishing your life had been something different or better.

High achievers are particularly prone to being in the GAP. For instance, research shows that CEOs are twice as likely to have depression than the general public.[4] Entrepreneurs are prone to substance abuse, as well as depression and suicide.[5] Even after some massive victory, their mind quickly goes to the next unreached achievement. Although this can lead to a great deal of external success, the problem remains unresolved internally. Many—if not most—high achievers remain unhappy, and their unhappiness grows deeper and deeper with each external accomplishment.

That is, if they stay in the GAP.

Thomas Jefferson was, of course, a very inspiring and significant person to American's history. But the fact remains: *Jefferson was in the GAP.*

And that's why he never "found" the happiness he was pursuing.

Unfortunately, Jefferson's GAP-thinking has become pervasive throughout Western ideology and thinking.

An example of GAP-thinking is a successful but unhappy man named Edward.

Edward is a former client of Chad Willardson, the founder and president of Pacific Capital, a premier wealth management firm in Southern California.

Back in early 2003, during his first meeting with Edward, Chad could tell by his body language that Edward had anxiety and worry. Edward mentioned that he was concerned about the stock market and where the economy was headed. Chad assured him that with the right team, plan, and strategy, his financial future would be secure and abundant.

After learning about Edward's financial situation, Chad further confirmed that Edward had every reason to be confident in his future. At that time, Edward was in his early 40s and had a multi-six-figure income with $2.5 million in cash to invest.

He told Chad, "If I can just get my investment portfolio to $5 million, then I'd feel secure financially and finally be able to relax."

They set Edward's goal at $5 million.

Edward followed the plan he and Chad had developed. He was adding money every year to his accounts and his investments were growing and compounding excellently.

Within a few years, he passed his original goal of having $5 million in his investment portfolio. But once he got there, he still didn't feel secure.

He was in the GAP.

He was worried about the future.

"I feel like I need $10 million to really feel safe and secure," he told Chad.

With his great income and investment strategy, his portfolio eventually did grow beyond $10 million, and by 2019, his portfolio was up to $17 million—over three times his original financial freedom target.

From an outside perspective, this man was more than living the American dream. He had grown to have a seven-figure income. He had a huge nest egg of compounding assets. And without question, he was a savvy and smart businessman.

Yet, he never outgrew his GAP-mindset. He never learned how to appreciate his GAINS. He was never grateful or happy about his situation.

He remained anxious and worried about the future. He continued to consume GAP-media that convinced him the financial world was going to collapse, and that he was going to lose all his money.

He requested a meeting with Chad. He wanted to abandon the planning and strategy that they'd been successfully executing over the previous 16 years and go completely conservative into cash. His view of the future was pessimistic. He didn't anticipate any more future growth.

Given that Edward was abandoning the plan and strategy Chad was providing and executing, it was clear they were no longer aligned. They decided to go their separate ways.

Edward sold off his investments and put all of his GAP-money into the bank, where it has sat since early 2019 when they had that conversation. At the writing of this book in mid-2021, the S&P Index has grown over 68% in the 2 years since Edward fearfully took his money out of the market.

Edward couldn't escape the GAP.

Edward couldn't appreciate his GAINS.

He was always trying to bridge a GAP he believed was somewhere in his future.

But the hard fact is that the GAP was always deep *inside himself.* Eventually, his GAP-thinking became so extreme that he stopped believing in his future entirely.

It's a sad tale.

But even more sad is how common it is.

You too may have fallen for this GAP-mindset.

Maybe you too, like Thomas Jefferson and Edward, have continually reserved "happiness" and "success" for your future, but never your present.

If so, ***you will never "find" happiness.***

Despite your continually growing success, happiness and security will never be yours because the GAP-mindset eventually stops growth altogether.

If you're in the GAP and think that "happiness" and "success" are something you "pursue" and will have in your future, then you're in trouble.

You're making yourself miserable.

And just as bad, you're actually making everyone around you miserable with your GAP-thinking.

When you're in the GAP, you see everything though your GAP-lens. Nothing is ever enough. Nothing ever *will* be enough. You can't see the GAIN in yourself or others. And until you do, you'll never be happy. Plain and simple.

Jefferson was wrong.

Happiness is not in the future.

If you're ready to finally get out of the GAP, then you're about to learn how. This book will show you the ONLY way out of the GAP. And luckily for you, it's incredibly simple. But don't be fooled by the simplicity of what you're about to learn.

It's human nature to be in the GAP.

The GAIN is the antidote.

The GAIN creates immediate happiness.

The GAIN connects you to yourself and your own progress.

The GAIN transforms everything.

The GAIN gives you power over the direction in your life.

The GAIN gets you out of the GAP.

On the day Dan discovered the GAP, he was frustrated by one of his clients, Bob (not his real name), who was himself frustrated and thus creating negative energy among the rest of the group.

A fundamental aspect of Strategic Coach, Dan's coaching program, is having his entrepreneurial clients meet every 60–90 days. While they meet, the entrepreneurs go through thinking tools that allow them to reflect, strategize, and get unique and helpful perspectives for their lives and businesses.

Dan asked Bob what he had accomplished in the previous 90 days, and Bob started sharing some of the progress his company had made, such as a new deal they'd secured.

But immediately after sharing what they'd done, Bob began explaining that their "progress" didn't actually mean anything, because it wasn't what could have or should have happened.

"Yeah, but none of that really means anything because . . . "

While listening to Bob devalue his progress and complain about his situation, Dan suddenly and clearly saw an explanation for a weird thing that successful entrepreneurs do to undermine their growth and confidence. This wasn't the first time he'd heard one of his clients grumble about their progress.

Dan walked to his paper flip chart and drew a picture to explain to Bob what was happening.

At the top of the paper, Dan wrote the word *Ideal.*

At the bottom of the page, he wrote *Start.*

Then between the two words, on the middle of the page, he wrote *Achieved.*

He then drew a line between the words *Achieved* and *Ideal.*

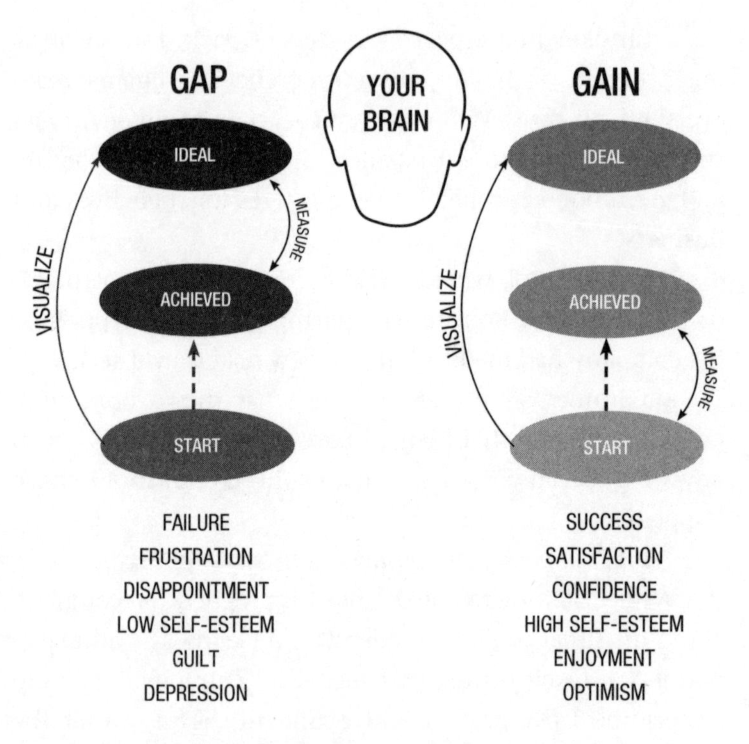

He explained it to Bob like this:

"The *Start* is where you were 90 days ago.

"The *Achieved* is what you've actually achieved over the past 90 days.

"The *Ideal* is where you wish you were.

"You have an ideal in your mind, and you're measuring yourself against your ideal, rather than against the actual progress you've made. This is why you're unhappy with what you've done, and it's probably why you're unhappy with everything in your life.

"You're measuring yourself in the GAP."

While drawing and thinking out loud, Dan unknowingly formulated what would become one of the most important, transformational, and enduring concepts in the Strategic Coach program.

But in that moment, it was just an unpolished insight. And Bob, the unhappy man Dan was talking to, didn't want to hear what Dan was saying. Instead, Bob stayed in the GAP, and started complaining about Dan's explanation, pointing out why and how it didn't apply to him.

Despite's Bob resistance, the other entrepreneurs in the room were completely blown away by what Dan was teaching them. They immediately observed how the GAP related to their own situations.

They could see how the GAP had permeated their lives, and that it was making them miserable.

You're in the GAP every time you measure yourself or your situation against an ideal.

For instance, you may be on your way to a concert with your spouse that you've been anticipating, but you're running five minutes late. If you're focused on and frustrated about those five minutes, *then you're in the GAP.*

You're measuring yourself against your ideal.

You're not actually living in the moment.

All you have to do is shift to the GAIN and focus on the fact that you're having an exciting night. *The whole night is a GAIN.*

If you focus on the GAIN, you'll be happy.

In every circumstance you're in, you're either in the GAP or the GAIN, but you can't be in both at once.

My wife, Lauren, makes home-cooked meals for dinner every night. Sometimes, our kids get to the table and complain that the meal isn't their favorite dish.

"Are you in the GAP or the GAIN?" I ask them.

They've heard it so many times at this point that sometimes it actually sinks in.

"Thanks for making dinner, mom."

The truth is, they've just GAINED, right?

They weren't appreciating the meal in front of them—or their lives for that matter—because they were measuring their experience against an ideal in that moment.

GET OFF THE GAP TREADMILL

> *"The day you stop racing is the day you win the race."*
>
> —Bob Marley

Measuring yourself against an ideal is an endless race to nowhere. That "ideal" could be in the form of a hope or expectation. It could be a comparison with something or someone else: *"Her raise was bigger than my raise."*

Being in the GAP stops you from living within your own experience. It stops you from appreciating where you are. It stops you from being happy.

As Greg McKeown put it:

> "If you focus on what you lack, you lose what you have. If you focus on what you have, you gain what you lack."[6]

When you're in the GAP, you lose what you have.

The GAP makes every experience a negative, which means you're worse off than you were before that experience.

The GAP makes any form of progress a letdown. Whatever you've done isn't enough because the "standard of success" keeps moving.

The GAP makes you a tyrant. All you can see is where others aren't measuring up.

Ideals are like a horizon in the desert. No matter how many steps you take forward, the horizon continues to move out of reach.

Psychology has a term for this moving horizon, *hedonic adaptation.* It's the tendency of humans to quickly adapt to where they are and what they've got. It leads to never being satisfied, and to constantly seeking the next thing.[7]

Hedonic adaptation is so powerful that no matter how big the change is—you marry your dream girl, double your income, or achieve all your goals—the thrill wears off and you quickly revert to feeling "normal" and unfulfilled again.[8]

You've moved forward and the horizon moved with you.

Psychologist Dr. Michael Eysenck gave another term to describe this phenomenon: "the hedonic treadmill."[9] When you're on this treadmill, you're working harder and harder to be happy but *staying exactly where you started.*

The reason the hedonic treadmill exists is because people aren't taught how to be happy. Ideals are meant to provide direction, motivation, and meaning to our lives.

They are not the measuring stick.

Our society has trained us to *measure ourselves against our ideals, which by definition are unreachable.*

Goals, conversely, are reachable.

But our society is driven by continually inflated and unreachable ideals. And that is why we live in a consumer-driven culture. It's why we're keeping up with the Joneses.

GOALS EXPAND HAPPINESS

"I don't think we set and achieve goals in an effort to become happy. We do it because we are happy and want to expand our happiness."

Even religion, which is supposed to bring people hope and healing, can be a reason people go into the GAP. As one friend told me, "I've always measured myself against perfection, because that's what I believe God can make me. And I'm never measuring up."

Maybe he didn't get the memo that God is in the GAIN, not the GAP.

Let's say your starting point is 1 and your goal is 30, but you only get to 22. You're in the GAIN if you focus on the actual progress you've made.

You're in the GAP if you're measuring yourself against that 30, so you are 8 short. If you're in the GAIN, you measure yourself against the 1, and see you've moved up 21 spots.

Being in the GAIN means you measure yourself backward, against where you were before.

You measure *your own* progress. You don't compare yourself to something external. You don't measure yourself against your ideals.

We all have countless experiences in life. The question is: Are we truly valuing those experiences? Or are we comparing our experiences to someone else's?

When you're in the GAIN, you value your experiences—*all of them.*

Every experience is viewed as a GAIN.

When you're in the GAIN, your life is based on your actions and results, not what could have or should have happened.

The GAIN is about real "measurables," not ideals. As performance coach Tim Grover has said, *"Winners don't have a to-do list. They have a 'done' list."*[10]

When you're in the GAIN, you focus on what you've actually done. You measure your GAINS and use those GAINS to create more and better GAINS in your future.

Every experience can be transformed into a GAIN.

Being in the GAIN makes you psychologically bulletproof. It doesn't matter what actually occurs, you can turn the experience into a GAIN.

Lose your leg in a car accident? Measure the GAIN. Turn it into a GAIN.

Your spouse cheats on you? Measure the GAIN. Turn it into a GAIN.

Your business fails? Measure the GAIN. Turn it into a GAIN.

You lose your money in a Ponzi scheme? Measure the GAIN. Turn it into a GAIN.

These may seem like extreme examples. But what you'll soon find is that any experience *can* be transformed into a GAIN.

As Dan explains:

> "I've discovered that when something very emotional happens to me, it stays with me until I've converted it into lessons. Before I knew this was the case, I could become paralyzed by negative experiences for long periods of time."[11]

It really doesn't matter what the experience was; the choice is fully yours in how you frame it—whether in the GAP or the GAIN.

Whenever you transform an experience into a GAIN—by creating new lessons, insights, or standards for yourself—you become better and your future becomes bigger.

An experience only becomes valuable and useful once you've transformed it into a GAIN.

Many people have lots of experience but very little learning.

When you're in the GAP about any experience, that experience becomes somewhat of a trauma to you. The word *trauma* may sound extreme, but trauma, by nature, is an experience you've framed as negative, which you avoid, and which creates ongoing dysfunction and debilitation in your life.

When an experience is framed in the GAP, you haven't learned from it. You haven't taken ownership of it. Until you actively learn from a GAP-experience, you're stuck. You won't be able to move forward until you frame the experience as a GAIN. Until you choose to be grateful for the experience and better off because it happened.

Once you get yourself in the GAIN, you become better.

You're no longer bitter.

You're grateful for every experience.

You're living your life based on your own success measurements—which you yourself have chosen.

You embrace "failing" (i.e., *learning*) because you're actively converting every experience into learning and growth—GAINS.

Seth Godin said:

> "The rule is simple: the person who fails the most will win. If I fail more than you do, I will win. Because in order to keep failing, you've got to be good enough to keep playing."[12,13]

Everything in life happens FOR you, not TO you.

Nothing can stop you so long as you transform every experience into a GAIN.

By defining your own measure of success, and by actively growing through your experiences, you'll continually be shocked by how far you've come.

You'll regularly look back at where you previously were and see accelerated growth.

You'll see increasingly tangible and measurable progress.

Your progress will be startling to most outsiders, because many people spend enormous amounts of time in the GAP, which means they aren't converting their experiences into learning. It means they aren't utilizing every experience to refine how they define and measure success.

When you're in the GAIN, you become unstoppable.

When you're in the GAIN, your progress becomes increasingly measurable to yourself and everyone around you.

Yet, the more you're in the GAIN, the less you compare, compete, or even care what other people think about you.

Being in the GAIN leads you to becoming increasingly unique and self-determined as a person. By no longer measuring yourself against externals, and by transforming every experience into a GAIN, you become a highly unique and incomparable person to anyone else.

You're playing your own game.

You're seeing new progress every day.

You're defining what your own experiences mean.

You're loving your life.

BE IN THE GAIN FOR OTHERS

"The meaning of life is whatever you ascribe it to be."

—JOSEPH CAMPBELL[14]

HAPPINESS IS YOUR STARTING POINT

"Happiness is your starting point, and you've expanded the center by achieving the goal. So, it's a constant outward expansion of happiness."

My name is Dr. Benjamin Hardy. I'm an organizational psychologist and best-selling author. I'm also the writer of this book and co-author with Dan Sullivan.

Together, Dan and I co-authored *Who Not How: The Formula to Achieve Bigger Goals Through Accelerating Teamwork.* That book was published in 2020 and became a national bestseller.

When you ask "Who?" rather than "How?" you free yourself of the burden of needing to do all the work yourself. Instead, you become a leader with vision and a team of capable "Whos" onboard to execute that vision.

This is why *I'm* the one writing this book and not Dan. He doesn't write these kinds of books, I do. Yet, he wants these books written. Rather than doing the "How" himself, Dan gets "Whos" to support his increasingly growing vision.

Strategic Coach is the #1 entrepreneurial coaching program in the world. Thousands of the world's top entrepreneurs get trained every 60–90 days by Strategic Coach.

Its mission is to increase entrepreneurial freedom, happiness, and success.

When you understand Dan's teachings and tools, success and freedom become inevitable. I can attest to this myself. I started learning from Dan in 2014 during the first year of my PhD program. Back then, I was making $12,000 per year as a graduate research assistant. Through Dan's teachings, I was able to create a seven-figure business and build a team before graduating. Since then, I've continued to apply *Who Not How* to create increasing results and freedom in my life.

But as excited as I was to share *Who Not How* with the world, I'm even more excited to share *The Gap and The Gain*. Having spent the past 12 years getting a PhD in psychology and reading over 1,000 books on the topic, I can say with conviction that I've never found a concept or framework as succinct, clear, and useful as *The GAP and The GAIN.*

Within this one simple concept is a master class on positive psychology, healthy relationships, mental well-being, and high performance. Everything that psychologists know about how to create a high-functioning and successful person can be achieved using *The GAP and The GAIN.*

It's the ultimate simplification, or what Dan would call an "intellectual shortcut."

Let me tell you right now why I wrote this book. When I first learned *The GAP and The GAIN,* I immediately started using it and it changed my life. It changed how I approach my work, my team, and, most importantly, my family.

As a family, we reference *The GAP and The GAIN* every single day. My kids even call me out when they catch me going into the GAP (which is more often than I'd like to admit).

I'm about to share something very personal: I hate who I am when I'm in the GAP. When I'm in the GAP about my kids—especially the older three we adopted from the foster system a few years back—I instill an enormous amount of psychological damage in them.

When you're in the GAP about someone else, all you see is where they're not measuring up.

You only see their flaws.

You don't see their GAINS or growth.

Take, for example, my oldest son. He's an incredible young man. We first met him as a 7-year-old boy living in a group home. He's been living with us ever since, and he's one of my favorite people.

Every once in a while, he tries to weasel his way out of chores or schoolwork. This may be typical for a young child, but this has been a trigger for me, and when I see him doing it, I can get pretty frustrated with him.

"Why are you always trying to get out of stuff?!" I bark at him.

He shuts down emotionally when I do this.

He later told me it feels like I only see his faults.

When I'm in the GAP about my son, I'm measuring him against *where I wish he was as a person*. I'm measuring his behavior against my ideals. By seeing my son through the lens of the GAP, all I can see are his flaws. I don't see him for who he truly is, right now.

I don't see his growth.

I don't see his progress.

When I measure him thoughtfully right now against where he was when we first met him, *it's incredible how much progress he's made*. Not only intellectually, but emotionally, physically, and in all other ways. It's actually crazy how much he's grown and changed.

But if I'm in the GAP, *I see none of that*. The only thing I see is where he's not measuring up against my continually changing ideals.

If I'm in the GAP, I become a tyrant and a bully to my son, rather than his biggest fan and supporter.

And that's why *The GAP and The GAIN* is central to my life. I've learned to focus on the GAINS. To vocalize those GAINS. To point them out to my son and to everyone around me.

When you focus on the GAIN, you and everyone around you are transformed.

Throughout this book you will find additional thoughts from Dan Sullivan in the form of full-page quotes.

IDEALS ILLUMINATE THE PATH

"The ideal is like the sun that illuminates the path ahead of you to give you the encouragement to take the necessary steps to reach your destination."

PART I

GET OUT OF THE GAP

CHAPTER 1

EMBRACE THE FREEDOM OF "WANTS"

Avoid the Attachment of "Needs"

"You, and you alone, are the person who should take the measure of your own success. I do not try to be better than anyone else. I only try to be better than myself."

—Dan Jansen

Dan Jansen is considered by many to be the best speed skater to ever live. By the young age of 16, he competed and very nearly won a medal in the 1984 Winter Olympics. Over the following decade, it became clear to everyone who followed speed skating that Jansen was the *most talented* skater on the planet.

But he seemed to be jinxed.

In his biggest races, he would start out at world-record-breaking speeds. But then something always seemed to happen that stopped him from winning. Little things.

Fluke things. It was widely believed that he deserved to be an Olympic medalist.

During the 1994 Olympics, Jansen had his final realistic shot at winning an Olympic medal. In his strongest event, the 500-meter, he finished eighth and was heartbroken. It didn't look like he was ever going to get his Olympic medal after all.

He had one final event, the 1,000-meter, which he'd previously considered his weakest event.

Before the race, Jansen decided to compete with a completely new mindset.

Rather than being in the GAP and thinking about the medal he needed in order to feel successful, and remembering all the races he *should've* won but didn't, he decided instead to be in the GAIN and focus on everything great in his life.[1]

He thought about the coaches who poured endless energy and care into him.

His family who loved him.

His friends who supported him.

All of the amazing experiences and blessings he had.

The fact that he'd become one of the best speed skaters of all time.

He even thought about his love for skating itself, and how much skating had done for him as a person.

He found himself in tears and overwhelmed by just how much he'd GAINED throughout his life, and as a skater.

With this reflection, he was able to comprehend how fortunate he was to even be in this situation at all. *He was skating in the Olympics!*

By appreciating the GAINS in his life, Jansen was deeply humbled.

He decided this final Olympic event would be an *expression of gratitude*—a way of saying "thank you" and "goodbye" to the sport, the people, and the experiences he loved so much.

At that point, it didn't really matter if he won or lost.

He was overcome with joy and gratitude, and he decided to skate with all of the GAINS in his life *as his motivation*.

Throughout the race, he was beaming a huge smile. He later said it was the happiest he'd ever skated in his whole life.

That run broke a world record and was one of the most emotional wins in Olympic history. Jansen skated near-flawlessly and won the gold.

He won his only Olympic medal in this, his final event. It was the first race he'd ever skated in the GAIN instead of the GAP.

Happiness is not something you pursue.

Happiness is not somewhere in the future.

Decades of scientific research is clear on this point: **happiness is *where you start*, not where you finish.**[2]

Take, for example, the *broaden-and-build theory* of psychology first introduced by Dr. Barbara L. Fredrickson, which shows that positive emotions are the starting point of learning, growth, and high performance.[3]

Positive emotions *broaden* your options of thinking and acting. As an example, research shows that people in high-stakes situations make the best choices when in a state of gratitude. They can see more clearly the best option before them.[4] On the flip side, negative emotions narrow your options, leaving you with only a few rigid ways of handling a given situation.

With a broadened mindset, you can then *build* new "resources" that you can use now or in the future—whether they be fresh perspectives, increased emotional flexibility, new strategies, or new relationships.

Positive emotions facilitate higher performance, which increases confidence and filters back more positive emotions. It's a virtuous cycle.

Dan Jansen tapped into the *broaden-and-build* phenomenon as he shifted from the GAP to the GAIN. By focusing on the GAINS in his life, he immediately *felt better* about his life. In fact, he started to feel overwhelmed with joy and gratitude. These positive emotions made him more flexible and creative during his race. He raced with joy and he raced better than he ever had before.

Being in the GAIN expanded and transformed Jansen.

But there's more. Research in psychology shows that confidence is not what creates success, but rather, prior success is actually what creates confidence.[5] While in the GAP and thinking about the races he should have won but didn't, Jansen was unwittingly killing his own confidence levels, which would have negatively impacted his final performance.

However, by focusing on the GAINS in his life, and by looking back on everything he'd achieved, his confidence levels immediately elevated. That confidence enabled him to believe even deeper that he could win and deepened his focus and drive during that gold medal victory.

All he had to do was think about his GAINS.

That was his way out of the GAP.

By focusing on his GAINS, he felt amazing. He felt confident. He felt grateful. He was in a peak state and performed at a higher level than he ever had previously.

Referencing your GAINS to boost confidence doesn't just apply to sports.

REALITY MEASURED BACKWARD

"The future isn't a reality—it's a projection. And because it's not reality, it can't be part of any real measurement of your progress. The only way to measure goals is backward, against the past. Use the reality of where you currently are and measure backward from there to the reality of where you started."

Kate Dewhirst is an accomplished health care lawyer in Toronto, Canada. She has the tough job of helping health care practitioners learn and become compliant with the ever-changing legal system, which they often see as overly complex and a distraction from their goal of helping their clients.

Kate always starts by helping them see their past GAINS, and that they've learned and applied the law in the past to their benefit. By helping them see that *"they've done this before"* in some fashion, they expand their confidence and willingness to learn.

Kate leverages her own past GAINS to spark confidence in herself whenever she feels resistance toward reaching a higher level personally or professionally.

Seeing her GAINS is how she's rapidly advancing her life and career.

Back to Jansen.

Perhaps the most important by-product of being in the GAIN was that Jansen no longer "needed" to win. Sure, he wanted to win. He was committed to performing his best. But he no longer "needed" that gold medal in order to feel worthy or successful.

Winning the gold medal could not have made Dan Jansen happy if he felt he *needed* it to be happy or to feel successful.

Needing anything outside of yourself is a form of being in the GAP.

When you're in the GAP, your happiness is tied to something outside of yourself, a moving and unreachable target.

When you're in the GAP, you have an unhealthy attachment to something external.

You feel you *need* something outside of yourself in order to be whole and happy.

You *need* to have a million dollars.

You *need* that person's approval.

You *need* that position or promotion.

You *need* to be a particular size or shape or to look a certain way.

When you're driven by need, rather than want, you have an urgency and desperation to fulfill that need. The problem is that "needs" are *unresolved internal pain,* not something you can solve externally.

Bill Wilson, the co-founder of Alcoholics Anonymous, said, "All progress starts by telling the truth."

But when you're in the GAP, you avoid looking inside. You avoid facing the truth that you're miserable. Instead, you continually search and seek outwardly to fill the GAP inside.

By focusing on the GAIN in his life, Jansen was happy and successful *before* winning the gold. He didn't *need* that medal to make him happy. He was already there.

He was already successful.

If he hadn't won, *he still would have been happy and successful.* Losing that race could not have made him a failure.

He decided that his life was filled with GAINS.

As the famed entrepreneur and investor Naval Ravikant said:

> "Training yourself to be happy is completely internal. There is no external progress, no external validation. You're competing against yourself—it is a single-player game."[6]

Happiness cannot come from something outside of yourself.

NO SCARCITY WITH WANTING

"In the world of wanting, there's no scarcity, because it's a world of innovation—not of taking. Wanters are creating things that didn't exist before."

Happiness is a byproduct of realizing that *you* are the destination.

You are enough and you have enough.

You are worthy of love.

Your viewpoints and judgments of your own experiences are infinitely more important than anyone else's judgments of you and of your experiences.

By now, you should be able to identify the GAP in some areas of your life. If you're human, then you've been in the GAP at least a handful of times even today.

Let's get practical. Throughout this book, there will be several exercises and journal prompts to help you get out of the GAP and into the GAIN. Start by grabbing a piece of paper and answering the following questions:

- What do you feel you "need" in order to be happy?
- Who or what do you measure yourself against?
- When is a time in your life where you made something or someone into a "need," and thus created an unhealthy GAP in your life?

OBSESSIVE VS. HARMONIOUS PASSION

"The difference between the two words 'need' and 'want' is gargantuan. When you need someone, you lose your independence and agency as a human being. Wanting, on the other hand, is the first step in learning how to love someone. The difference between need and want is the difference between codependence and love."

—MICHAELA ROLLINGS, POPULAR BLOGGER[7]

In an April 2021 interview with *Sports Illustrated,* Trevor Lawrence, the Clemson quarterback and projected #1 NFL draft pick said he didn't "need" football to feel worthy as a person, and that there is "more to life than football."

Trevor's coach at Cartersville High, Joey King, said, "There is no doubt about it: With who he is as a person, he could walk away from it tomorrow and be fine."

The response throughout the NFL and media world was hysterical. Every major sports channel and even mainstream news covered the story. Trevor's comments were shocking from someone with his record. Trevor had 52 wins and 2 losses as a high school five-star recruit, and 34 wins and 2 losses as one of the most elite college quarterbacks ever.

"He must not be a true competitor."

"This is not the type of mindset of someone who is going to win in this league."

"If Trevor Lawrence isn't 100% obsessed about football, then he will not win at this level."

"I don't know how great you can really be if you're not selfish and adopt the win-at-all-costs attitude." [8]

There's a common perception that in order to be the best at what you do, you've got to be completely obsessed with what you're doing. You've got to "NEED" your passion with every fiber of your being. Essentially, you've got to be unhealthy about whatever it is if you want to truly be great at it.

Trevor Lawrence rubbed the whole sports world the wrong way because he basically said, "No, I don't," to the idea that he "needed" football in an unhealthy and obsessive way in order to be the best.

The story and media were getting so out of hand and over-the-top that Trevor decided to clarify his comments on Twitter.[9] He said:

> "It seems as if people are misreading my sentiment. I am internally motivated—I love football as much or more than anyone. It is a HUGE priority in my life, obviously. I am driven to be the best I can be, and to maximize my potential. And to WIN. . . .
>
> "I have a lot of confidence in my work ethic, I love to grind and to chase my goals. You can ask anyone who has been in my life. That being said, I am secure in who I am, and what I believe. I don't need football to make me feel worthy as a person. I purely love the game and everything that comes with it."

A few days after the media explosion and Trevor's Twitter response, he appeared on *ESPN's First Take* show with reporter Stephen A. Smith to further discuss the matter.[10]

> "I don't feel like I have anything to prove because that's not how I operate. I'm internally motivated. . . . I've got goals, aspirations, dreams to be the best I can be. And it's really just a love of the game.
>
> "That was the message: I just love playing the game. I'm not motivated by other people. It's really just an internal motivation, and I don't put my whole worth in football. . . .
>
> "If football went away, I'd find something else to do and I'd still have a great life and enjoy my life. But football is where my heart's at. It's what I love to do. It's what I've loved to do since I was six years old. This has been my dream forever. And I really believe no one works harder than me.
>
> ***"I think you can have both.*** People want it to be one or the other. But for me, that's what's been one of the healthiest things is realizing that this isn't the

> only thing in the world. There's more to it, but also, football has been the biggest priority in my life. . . .
>
> ***"I play the long-game.*** . . . I'm putting all my eggs in the basket of me performing well and living up to the expectations I have for myself, not what other people have for me."

Trevor Lawrence demonstrated at a deep internal level how both happiness AND high performance work.

Here's the reality: not only is Trevor Lawrence healthy and happy as an individual, but research proves that his is the optimal mindset for maximizing his potential as a high performer.[11,12]

The fact that his comments were so misunderstood by the media and sports world is a clear evidence that *most people*—even highly successful people—do not understand how both happiness AND high performance work.

Most high performers or "successful" people never took the class on happiness. And there's a thick narrative out there that in order to be the best performer you can be, "happiness" and "balance" cannot be part of the equation.

But that conventional wisdom is wrong. Putting yourself in the GAP is not how you reach your highest level.

Having an unhealthy "need" or "obsession" is not how you reach your highest level.

Trevor Lawrence was dead-on in his perspectives—and he was completely misunderstood and chastised as a result.

Consider Trevor's words: "I think you can have both." What he meant by "both" is:

1. Having an intense commitment to succeed, and
2. Having a healthy detachment from what you're doing

WANTING IS A CAPABILITY

"This transformation, moving from needing to wanting, is a capability. The more you do it, the better you get at it. Yes, it's a risk at first because your previous tendencies of justification are well developed and habitual."

As he stated, he loves football. He works hard. He's committed to winning. *But he doesn't need football.*

That's his point—you can have both: you can be 100% committed to something and simultaneously not need it.

When you're in the GAP, you "need" something outside of yourself. You're driven externally. You're reactive to what's going on outside of you.

In the GAIN, you don't "need" anything outside of yourself. You're driven internally. You take what happens outside of you to transform and improve yourself.

Being in the GAP is driven by an unhealthy "need."

Being in the GAIN is driven by a healthy and chosen "want."

Psychologists have separated needs and wants into two core types of passion: *obsessive and harmonious.*[13]

Obsessive passion is highly impulsive and fueled by suppressed emotions and unresolved internal conflict. You become obsessed with something to the point of an unhealthy desperation. You believe you *need* it, and can't be happy without it.

Obsessive passion is regularly associated with addiction. Also, when you become obsessively passionate about something, you lose sight of the other areas of your life. Your obsession takes over and you sabotage the other areas of your life by making short-sighted decisions to get what you're obsessing about.

The moment you become obsessive or attached to something, you're in the GAP.

This could be in big or small things.

If you have the need to be "right" in an argument, then you're in the GAP.

If something doesn't go how you planned and you're upset, you're in the GAP.

You're measuring your experience or situation against how you ideally imagined it was "supposed" to be, rather than learning from the experience and being happy regardless.

Research shows that obsessive passion stops you from being mindful.[14,15]

You have a difficult time being in the moment because you're so fixated on your obsession. It's all-consuming, but also filled with twinges of regret and internal conflict.

Hence, obsessive passion actually stops you from being in a flow state—or the state of being fully immersed in what you're doing.[16] Instead, with obsessive passion, you're disconnected from yourself and those around you.

Furthermore, obsessive passion is correlated with low self-esteem.[17] If you feel like you "need" something in order to be whole or happy as a person, then clearly you don't think you're enough here and now. You're in the GAP about yourself, and are trying to fill that GAP obsessively and unhealthily.

Trevor Lawrence isn't trying to fill a GAP by being successful or famous as a football player. As he stated, he's already worthy and happy even without football. He lives in the GAIN.

Harmonious passion, on the other hand, is intrinsically motivated and healthy. When you are harmoniously passionate, you control your passion rather than having it control you. You're intuitive and thoughtful about what you're doing, not reactive and irrational. You're purposeful and goal-directed, not "need"-driven.

WANTING EMPOWERS YOU

"When you take the wanting approach to your future, it also means that you're leaving behind the world of needing. It means that no one else is responsible for your future progress and success."

You can know a passion is harmonious if it *enhances the other key aspects of your life*, and if it makes you better as a person. Harmonious passion is related to being in a flow state.[18] Being in a flow state stems from intrinsic motivation—a core aspect of harmonious passion—where you're performing for the sake of the passion, rather than as a means to an end.[19,20,21]

Trevor Lawrence loves football for the sake of it. As he stated over and over, he's intrinsically, not extrinsically, motivated to play football. He's not trying to prove himself to anyone else.

If he was playing football to prove himself to other people, or to feel good about himself, or even to be happy—then he'd be in the GAP. He'd have an unhealthy need.

Instead, Trevor Lawrence has a healthy and harmonious passion toward football that is intrinsically motivated. He loves playing the game. He's got his own standards and expectations for himself, which are likely *much higher* than many others playing in the league.

He decides his own measure of success.

He decides how far he can go.

He controls his passion.

This brings up a highly nuanced and crucial distinction: you can want something and be 100% committed to that thing *without needing it.*

This is the counterintuitive reality: by no longer *needing* what you want, you are actually far more enabled to get it.

You can freely perform and be in the flow, rather than obsessing over how it will turn out.

Once Dan Jansen stopped *needing* that gold medal, and once he started appreciating all of his GAINS, then and only then could he skate and perform at a higher level than he ever had before.

PLAY THE LONG GAME

In psychology, *grit* is defined as passion and perseverance toward long-term goals.[22] Harmonious passion is related to having high levels of grit, whereas obsessive passion is not.[23]

If you're obsessively passionate, you're thinking short-term. You're trying to force things to go your way. But you don't truly want whatever it is you're seeking. You just think you need it because you're unresolved internally. Whether you get what you want or not, sooner or later you'll shift that unhealthy need onto something else—the hedonic treadmill will continue.

Similar to harmonious passion, intrinsic motivation is also related to having high levels of grit, whereas extrinsic motivation is not.[24]

When you're doing something you genuinely love, and you're doing it *for yourself,* then you're intrinsically motivated and have a healthy passion.

You don't need to "force" things or "prove" yourself.

You're playing the long game.

You're playing *your own game.*

You're not competing with anyone else.

You're not measuring yourself against anyone else's standards.

Something Dan Sullivan has noticed in coaching tens of thousands of entrepreneurs since 1974—*over 47 years!*—is that most of them are mentally "here" but wanting to be "there."

It really doesn't matter where they are now and how great their lives are, they continually wish they were "there."

Many high achievers have a hard time being "here." And although it's great to have goals and vision and be driven, you're in the GAP if you're "here" but wishing you were "there."

Playing a longer game allows you to embrace being "here." Yes, you have goals and vision, but you're completely happy where you're at.

You're *here,* and you love being here.

You love what your life is like.

You're blown away by your GAINS.

You appreciate everything and everyone around you.

You're genuinely happy.

You also love what you're working on and building. You're committed and focused, but you're not trying to rush to the next place to fill some unresolved need. You're doing what you love. You're confident in where your life is going.

Being "here" doesn't mean you don't have goals or aspirations.

Quite the contrary.

By freeing yourself from unnecessary "needs," you're finally enabled to create the progress and life *you* want.

You know you're already whole and complete without those goals.

You're fully free to have whatever you want, and because of that, it's actually much easier to get what you want.

As the American author Florence Shinn wrote, "Faith knows it has already received and acts accordingly."[25]

You're already "there," because you're completely at peace and want to be "here."

This "here wanting to be there" insight was particularly life-changing for my wife, Lauren, and I. As a highly motivated and goal-oriented person, I often find myself "here" but wishing I was "there." I've had a hard time truly appreciating my progress and being present to my life and family.

But after learning about *The GAP and The GAIN* from Dan, I realized I was in the GAP, a lot.

I was operating out of need, rather than want.

I felt I needed to get to the "next achievement" in order to be happy and successful.

This obsessiveness and external motivation had led to a great deal of achievement, but I wasn't happy. I wasn't pursuing the most aligned goals and priorities. I was still trying to prove myself. I was also disconnected from myself and those who mattered most to me.

One night, Lauren and I had a conversation about me being "here" but wanting to be "there." We live in Orlando, Florida, and have six kids. Our older three kids are 13, 11, and 9. In my mind, we would live in Orlando for the next 2–3 years until I reached a certain place in my career, and then we'd move on to the next place. When we moved here, in my mind it was a temporary spot.

After thinking about the "here wanting to be there" idea, I asked Lauren what she thought would be best for our family. She felt it would be best if we stayed here in Orlando until our 9-year-old was 18 years old and finished with high school.

As I contemplated that idea, it felt like an eternity. *Could I really stay in this house and continue doing what I'm doing for another 9 years, until 2030?* I thought to myself.

I gave myself permission to let go of needing to be "there."

What if I was completely here for the next 9 years? I thought.

WANTING CREATES ABUNDANCE

"In the wanting world, there is an abundance of resources as a result of the creativity and innovation that comes from wanting."

Wow. I'd never felt so *free*. This is where I *want* to be. I can fully be here and do what I'm doing, and see how far I can expand being here. I don't have to try getting "there" anymore.

I am here.

I love where I'm at.

I'm in the GAIN.

I know I can keep creating GAINS.

When you're in the GAP, you're desperate to get "there," because you're *trying to escape* being here. You're bouncing around, rather than getting real and getting traction.

When you're in the GAP, you aren't thinking long-term. You're impulsively trying to fill an unresolved "need."

Conversely, when you're in the GAIN, you no longer need to be "there." This doesn't mean you don't have huge goals. It simply means you're fully "here." You're where you want to be. You're playing a long game, which means you LOVE where you're at now, and you love where you're going.

You're here. You don't need to get "there."

You're here. *Be here.*

By playing the long game, you set your own course. You stop worrying about what other people think about you. You stop seeking other people's approval of how you're living your life. You stop trying to measure up to other people's standards of success.

Instead, you decide what success means to you, and you choose the life you'll live. You realize that you're living that life now.

You're free to live whatever life you want.

The GAIN creates freedom.

The GAP makes you a slave to your unhealthy need.

The GAP makes you a slave to "there" and makes "here" a prison you're trying to escape from.

Alright, it's time for another quick exercise. Pull out your journal and answer the following questions:

- Are there any areas in your life where you have obsessive passion? If so, what unresolved internal need are you trying to fill?
- What about your life and work do you love?
- *What is your long game?* When you're playing the long game, you're doing what you love. You're not doing something just to get somewhere else.
- Do you have a long enough time table to truly slow down and enjoy being here, or are you trying to quickly get "there"?
- Look at your life right now—what are all the GAINS you can think of?
- How would your priorities change if you were playing the long game?

FREEDOM "FROM" VS. FREEDOM "TO"

"Freedom is now or never."

—Jiddu Krishnamurti

In the classic book *Escape from Freedom,*[26] Erich Fromm defines two types of freedom:

1. *Freedom from* (which is external)
2. *Freedom to* (which is internal)

To be *free from* is to be no one's slave, to live in a free country, to have no coercion or force against you. It means you have no external restraints—such as hunger, the elements, and unjust laws—on your individual choice or behavior.[27]

To be *free to* is to be able to choose for yourself. You have the capability to choose. You have a variety of options from which to choose. You also have the courage to choose.[28]

You are the one who controls and directs your own life as you see fit.

You take full ownership.

You're not looking to someone or something outside of yourself.

You exercise free will and choice.

You act based on want, not need. For example, *freedom from* is external—you're free from hunger. *Freedom to* is internal—you're free to choose what you'll eat.

Freedom from is lack of obstacles—**you're not a slave** to someone or something.

Freedom to is the presence of control—**you're your own master.**

Freedom from is *objective and external*—you have objective freedom if you live in a free place. For example, an elephant out in the wild may have more external freedoms than an elephant living in a zoo.

Freedom to is *subjective and internal*—you have subjective freedom if you *feel free.*

Compared to other countries in the world, America has a great deal of freedoms afforded its citizens—although it is obviously not perfect.

Yet, despite having an enormous amount of *freedom from* constraints, it can be difficult to courageously seize the *freedom to* be whoever you genuinely want to be.[29] There are a lot of expectations and ideals to live up to in America, which can hamper intrinsic motivation.

These build on top of each other. *Freedom from* means you've removed the external obstacles. *Freedom to* asks, "Okay, what will you do now?"

The goal of creating an environment of freedom is that as an individual, you actually live your life according to your own choosing rather than compulsion.

Sadly, very few people are willing to take the leap into the higher level of freedom.

Psychologist Abraham Maslow's hierarchy of needs is another expression of freedom.[30] The lower levels of Maslow's hierarchy are *freedom from*–based—such as freedom from hunger, dangers, the elements, social isolation, and even lack of self-esteem.

Self-actualization, the highest level on Maslow's hierarchy, is another way of saying that you have the *freedom to* be whatever it is you choose to be.

You're completely *free,* which according to Maslow is the highest and noblest aim and desire of all humans.

You've freed yourself from internal and external constraints that would stop you from having autonomy and choice. The question you now must ask is:

What will you choose?

What do you want?

When you're in the GAP, you're not operating out of freedom and choice. Instead, you're operating from a position of lack or need.

IDEALS AREN'T FOR MEASUREMENT

"An ideal can't be measured. It's there for emotional, psychological, and intellectual motivation, but it's not there for measurement."

To restate, being in the GAP means you're still trying to free yourself FROM something. You're trying to fill a GAP.

The GAIN gives you freedom.

You must choose to be *freed from* the GAP. That's the first step we're inviting you to take in this book.

Free yourself FROM the GAP.

Free yourself from lack or need.

You can never have autonomy and agency until you free yourself from the GAP.

You'll never feel successful until you get out of that black hole.

Once you're out of the GAP, you're at the "freedom to" stage, where you can truly be whoever it is you want to be.

You're in the GAIN.

CHAPTER TAKEAWAYS

- The GAP is based on an unhealthy "need" or attachment to something outside of yourself.
- The GAP means you're still trying to free yourself FROM something, and until you do you won't be happy.
- When you're in the GAP, you're avoiding "here" while trying to get "there"—but never actually arriving "there."
- The GAIN is based on being in harmony with what you *want,* and knowing that you don't need it.

- When you're in the GAIN, you live your life based on intrinsic motivation and harmonious passion, which creates flow and high performance.
- When you're in the GAIN, you're completely free and happy right now. This enables you to commit 100 percent and pursue what you want without unhealthy attachments.

CHAPTER 2

BE SELF-DETERMINED

Define Your Own Success Criteria

"Define success on your own terms, achieve it by your own rules, and build a life you're proud to live."

—ANNE SWEENEY, AMERICAN BUSINESSWOMAN AND FORMER CO-CHAIR OF DISNEY MEDIA

One of mine and Lauren's friends is a senior getting ready to graduate from high school. She's taking five AP (advanced placement) classes, submitting her art to prestigious art competitions, and losing sleep every night stressing about getting "accepted" into a good school.

She's waiting to be "picked."

Her "measure of success" and "worth" as a person are being placed into the hands of people she doesn't know.

She's made getting accepted into a great college an obsessive and unhealthy "need" rather than a "want." If she doesn't get accepted into what she deems as a "great" school, she'll consign herself as a failure.

In other words: ***she's in the GAP.***

At 17 years old, she's glued to the hedonic treadmill.

Can she reverse this unhealthy striving?

Do public education and its "measures" breed success or compliance?

Seth Godin and many others have explained that public education was actually invented in 1918 to get kids out of the factories.[1],[2] Back then, kids as young as seven did grueling hard factory work. The education system was designed to train kids to be "better" and more obedient, productive, and submissive workers in the future.

The goal of the education system was definitely NOT for those children to become leaders or creative thinkers, but to become people who did what they were told, looked for the "right answer," and did not think for themselves.

As Seth Godin explains:

> "Our current system of teaching kids to sit in straight rows and obey instructions isn't a coincidence—it was an investment in our economic future. The plan: trade short-term child labor wages for longer-term productivity by giving kids a head start in doing what they're told."

One obvious reason that our public education system may hinder creativity and autonomy is HOW success is measured.[3]

A "reference point" is a standard for evaluation and comparison. In school, each child is measured against the reference points of national averages on test scores. In other words, each child is measured against other children, and given a "percentile rank" of how they match up to other children their age.

PROGRESS MUST BE CONCRETE

"A sense that we're making progress toward our goals makes us happy. But to truly get the feeling of progress, we need to base it on concrete facts. When we set goals, we must be specific so we know when they're accomplished—usually, a number was reached or an event took place."

In any domain or situation, "success" is always measured against a particular reference point.

Being fixated on outside reference points puts you in the GAP. Being directed by your own internal reference points strengthens being in the GAIN.

Children are trained to measure themselves against *external* reference points. These reference points are not generally chosen by the child themselves, but by society and the education system.

As these children grow up, they're not taught how to determine their own reference point or "measure of success." Instead, they adopt the reference points that society deems as "success"—money, fame, social media likes, etc.

Because all of these reference points are external—and become increasingly based on unreachable ideals—people's lives become the desperate and failing race to "measure up" to external and changing ideals. Hence the hedonic treadmill so many spend their lives on, trying to measure up and "be happy."

Every one of us has reference points we use to measure ourselves. Pull out your journal and answer these questions:

- What are the reference points you measure yourself against?
- Why did you choose those particular reference points?
- How do you define and measure success for yourself?

Become Self-Determined

"To be free, you must be self-determined, which is to say that you must be able to control your own destiny in your own interests."

—Stanford Encyclopedia of Philosophy[4]

According to *self-determination theory*, a crucial aspect of motivation and thriving is autonomy.[5] The more independence and ownership you take for yourself, your circumstances, and your life, the more self-determined you will be.

Being self-determined means that *you've made yourself the reference point*, rather than measuring yourself against something external.

Being self-determined means you're intrinsically, not extrinsically, motivated. This doesn't mean you don't use externals as measurables—but you yourself choose those goals for yourself.

Being self-determined means that you've decided what success means to you, and you don't need anyone else's permission for what you want for yourself. You don't need to apologize for what you want.

It means you're clear on WHY you want what you want.

It means you're no longer competing with anyone else.

Being in the GAIN leads to self-determination.

Becoming self-determined is *very difficult* in today's world. The noise and distractions are relentless, making it nearly impossible to truly make yourself your own reference point, and to have an internal compass.

Beyond the conditioning of external comparisons and competing we get in public education, we now have technology that is literally designed to addict and control us.[6]

Social media is largely designed to put people into the GAP.

It's designed to create unhealthy needs around being accepted and "liked." Indeed, research has shown that social media and FOMO (i.e., fear of missing out) go hand in hand.[7] FOMO is characterized by the desire to stay continually connected with what others are doing. People are trained to constantly "need" to know how and what others are doing, and to have others know what they are doing.

HOW TO MEASURE GAINS

"You can't make a real measurement of your gains unless it's based on numbers achieved or events that have made a difference. It has to be quantifiable and verifiable."

This is a very destructive form of living in the GAP.

But here's something perhaps more disturbing than anything else about social media, and how it puts people into the GAP. When you're in the GAP, you're measuring yourself against external ideals or reference points. In most cases, these ideals are not consciously chosen by you. Social media is articulately designed to *subconsciously manipulate* people's identity, their desires, and their behaviors.

Put more directly, social media is designed to stop people from becoming self-determined.

A statement used to describe social media in the Netflix documentary *The Social Dilemma* is, "If you're not paying for the product, then you are the product."[8]

Expounding on this idea, Jaron Lainer, a computer scientist and virtual reality pioneer, stated the following in *The Social Dilemma*:

> "That's a little too simplistic. ***It's the gradual, slight, imperceptible change in your own behavior and perception that is the product.*** And that *is* the product. That's the only possible product. There is nothing else on the table that could possibly be called the product. That's the only thing there is for them to make money from. Changing what you do, how you think, who you are. It's a gradual change. It's slight. . . .
>
> "We've created a world in which online connection has become primary. Especially for younger generations. And yet, in that world, anytime two people connect, the only way it's financed is through a sneaky third person who's paying to manipulate those two people."

Billions of dollars are spent every day to manipulate and change your thoughts, desires, and behaviors. The reference points for your own success are being created *for you,* not by you. If you're not paying for the product, then your behavior change is the product.

The American motivational speaker Zig Ziglar said it well: "Your input determines your outlook. Your outlook determines your output, and your output determines your future."[9]

The more you're subtly influenced by externals, the more in the GAP you'll be.

The more you'll measure yourself against ideals.

The less you'll be self-determined.

Ninety percent of people use social media websites for the specific purpose of *comparing themselves with others,* and nearly 100 percent of those comparisons are "upward social comparisons," meaning people are comparing themselves with those they perceive to be "above" or "better than them."[10]

No wonder the more time you spend on social media, the less self-esteem you'll have and the more depressed you'll be.[11,12]

No wonder suicide and addiction rates are skyrocketing among teens and adolescents.[13] The majority of their lives are spent being compared to others by teachers, parents, peers, and even themselves.

Any form of social comparison puts you in the GAP.

Measuring yourself against someone else puts you in the GAP.

Competing with someone else puts you in the GAP.

All of these contradict self-determination and intrinsic motivation. Instead, when you're measuring yourself against others, you become externally determined and extrinsically motivated.

You lose your own identity.

You lose your own compass.

You're chasing the wrong ideals, which will be a continual GAP-race to nowhere.

Your happiness as a person is dependent on what you measure yourself against.

The antidote to being in the GAP is to measure yourself by the GAIN. More specifically, ***you measure your own GAINS***, rather than worrying about other people.

This is how you become self-determined: You have an internal reference point. You stop measuring yourself against others. You only measure yourself against yourself.

You measure the GAIN, not the GAP.

Sandi McCoy is someone who had to stop caring what other people thought of her. She had to learn how to define success for herself, measure her own progress, and become self-determined.

It's been a long road for Sandi. Over the past 6 years, she has gone from being morbidly obese at 400 pounds to losing over 240 pounds. She has used her social media platform to authentically share the struggles she continues to deal with, even after 4 years of maintaining her weight loss.

She often has people criticize her photos, calling her fat and making fun of her excess skin. She's learned to ignore the haters. She's learned that she needs to define success for herself, because even after all those GAINS, she can still go in the GAP by comparing her figure or weight against others.

As she said on her Instagram account:

> "There used to be a time where I based my success on what I thought others wanted from me. I felt like I was always letting everyone down. Especially when it came to losing weight. It wasn't until I decided to make a list of what I actually wanted in life that I was finally able to succeed on the goals I set for myself. . . .
>
> "Today I tracked my calories, cleaned the house, did my knee exercises, went for a walk, and played some kick ball. To some people, this might not sound like a successful day, but to me it is. Success is measured by you. No one else can set your happy meter."[14]

Sandi is right. You have to be the one who defines success for yourself. You determine what a "successful day" looks like for you.

Change your reference point to be internal, where you measure your own progress.

As a quick exercise, pull out your journal and answer the following questions:

- Are the reference points you measure yourself against external or internal?
- How often do you compare yourself to others?
- How much time do you spend on social media?
- Are you self-determined and free?

Define Your "Success Criteria"

> *"What preoccupies us is the way we define success."*
>
> —Arianna Huffington[15]

APPRECIATE PROGRESS FIRST

"Before you start the process with a new goal, make sure to recognize and appreciate the progress and achievements you've made so far."

Dean Jackson is a marketing expert and entrepreneur. Twenty years ago, Dean had an aha moment about the inherent problem with "seeking success." Specifically, he concluded that using the phrase "I'll be successful when..." led people to chasing the wrong forms of "success," and never actually getting the life they wanted.

Dean decided to flip the question to put success in the here and now. He asked himself, "I know I'm *being* successful when . . . " and came up with a list of 10 items:[16]

1. I can wake up every day and ask, "What would I like to do today?"
2. My passive revenue exceeds my lifestyle needs.
3. I can live anywhere in the world I choose.
4. I'm working on projects that excite me and allow me to do my best work.
5. I can disappear for several months with no effect on my income.
6. There are no whiny people in my life.
7. I wear my watch for curiosity only.
8. I have no time obligations or deadlines.
9. I wear whatever I want all the time.
10. I can quit anytime.

This list reflects Dean's personal success criteria. His measuring stick is his own creation. He is self-determined.

He references his list regularly, especially when presented with opportunities or when trying to make decisions. If it's clear that an opportunity would take away from or is in conflict with any of Dean's 10 principles, he says no.

Having his own success criteria allows Dean to make informed decisions based on his own definition of success. He uses his list to avoid FOMO. He's happy saying "No" to situations, relationships, or opportunities that don't fit the success criteria he's made for himself.

Give this a try for yourself.

Spend 20 to 30 minutes with no distractions writing down your answer to this question: "I know I'm *being* successful when . . ."

Be as honest with yourself as you possibly can.

No one else can define success for you.

Defining your own success criteria is how you become self-determined. This is how you develop an internal reference system. You decide how you will measure yourself.

Be flexible with this list.

View it like the draft of a book that can be edited and improved. Chances are, you'd define success differently now than you would have 5–10 years ago.[17]

That's a good thing!

Also true is that your future self will likely define success differently than you do now. Therefore, don't think you're stuck with the list you are about to come up with.

The main point is that you have your own success criteria to guide how you spend your time and what you do. Continually refine and improve your "success criteria" as you advance your perspectives and experiences.

You don't have to have 10 items on your list like Dean does. But I'll provide you with space for 10:

ELIMINATE JUSTIFICATION

"By eliminating justification, you recognize that all the energy you were spending comes back in the form of creativity, innovation, and cooperation."

You are *being* successful when . . .

1.
2.
3.
4.
5.
6.
7.
8.
9.
10.

Like Dean Jackson with his "I'm *being* successful when . . ." list, Lee Brower, a successful entrepreneur and gratitude expert whose teachings have been viewed by more than 100 million people, developed a list of six questions he uses as a filtering process for making high-quality decisions.

Here are Lee's six filtering questions, which also act as his personal success criteria:

1. Is this opportunity, person, expense, adventure, experience, relationship, commitment, etc., aligned with my values?
   (If the answer to this first question is "No," then Lee doesn't proceed to ask himself the remaining five questions. If, however, the answer to this first question is "Yes," then he continues his filtering process.)

2. Will this opportunity, etc., take advantage of my unique ability and make me even stronger? Will it lengthen my stride?
3. How will this opportunity, etc., benefit mankind? Is there a bigger cause or purpose that will benefit society?
4. Does this make sense financially?
5. Is this transactional or transformational? In other words, is this a stand-alone opportunity or a gateway opportunity?
6. If I say "Yes" to this opportunity, what then must I say "No" to?

As with Dean's criteria, these are *Lee's* own personal criteria for making decisions. The point isn't to adopt Dean's or Lee's success criteria, although by all means draw from them or steal them if you're inspired. Rather, the purpose of providing these lists is to get you thinking deeply about your own measurements.

A fundamental aspect of being in the GAIN is to live your life in a self-determined way. You stop living in the GAP and measuring yourself based on ideals, but rather live based on *clear measurables* that you yourself have chosen.

You then regularly use those criteria to make decisions and move your life forward. As you move forward, you regularly measure yourself backward to evaluate your own progress.

There's a quiet confidence that comes from running your own race, from no longer measuring or comparing yourself to others.

The philosopher Seneca called it *euthymia*, which means "That you're on the right path and not led astray by the many tracks which cross yours of people who are hopelessly lost."[18]

IDEALS AS INSPIRATION

"The best way to look at your ideals is as an infinite source of inspiration for creating goals. We are all like moviemakers, using our entire memory and imagination as raw material for casting a never-ending series of pictures out in front of us."

Use Your Filtering System to Go Further, Faster

"Use this rule if you're often over-committed or too scattered. If you're not saying 'HELL YEAH!' about something, say 'no.' When deciding whether to do something, if you feel anything less than 'Wow! That would be amazing! Absolutely! Hell yeah!'—then say 'no.'"

—Derek Sivers[19]

The British rowing team had not won a gold medal since 1912. By all measures, they didn't have a good rowing program.

Then something changed.

In anticipation of the 2000 Sydney Olympics, the team developed a useful filtering process that changed everything. They went from being an average rowing team to winning Olympic gold.

They developed a one-question filtering response to every single decision they made. This one question allowed them to measure every situation, decision, and obstacle—and to not get derailed where most people do.

With every decision or opportunity, every member of the team asked themselves: ***WILL IT MAKE THE BOAT GO FASTER?***

Example: you get invited to a late-night party the night before training. ***WILL IT MAKE THE BOAT GO FASTER?***

If the answer is no, then the decision is no.

Tempted to eat a donut? ***WILL IT MAKE THE BOAT GO FASTER?***

The British rowing team used this single measure as their decision filter to quickly escalate their unity, skills, conditioning, and training.

CREATE SUCCESS CRITERIA

"The simplest and most efficient way to ensure you get the results you want is to create a list of success criteria for your goals."

They destroyed their competition and won gold.

Like the British rowing team, your success criteria become more powerful and effective as you use them. A list of effective "success criteria" is something you can easily apply, especially in heated situations where you could compromise.

Get very good at saying "No" to anything that misaligns with your success criteria. As you do, you'll be shocked at the confidence and momentum you quickly build.

Your list of success criteria is your *rocket fuel.*

The more you live it and stay within it, the faster you'll get to where you want to go.

Time for a quick exercise. Pull out your journal and simplify the success criteria you've listed above.

- Are your success criteria focused on the outcomes you currently want?
- What's a simple filter you can create to assess every decision you make (e.g., "Will it make the boat go faster?")?
- What is one thing you can apply this filter to in the next 3 hours?

Chapter Takeaways

- External reference points make it impossible to feel successful because no matter what you've done, the success criteria are always moving.
- Getting out of the GAP and into the GAIN means you've made yourself your own reference point.

- The GAP means your life is determined by someone or something external. The GAIN means you're living a self-determined life.
- When your reference point is internal, you make the final call on what "success" means to you, regardless of what other people think.
- When your reference point is internal, happiness and success are always right here and right now.

BE SPECIFIC, NOT VAGUE

"Vagueness generates vagueness, so you must be specific when describing your desired results."

CHAPTER 3

THE COMPOUND EFFECT OF THE GAP OR GAIN

Train Your Brain to See GAINS

"Sometimes the greatest scientific breakthroughs happen because someone ignores the prevailing pessimism."

—NESSA CAREY, BRITISH BIOLOGIST[1]

The GAP stresses you out. It taxes and ages your physical body. It erodes your emotional well-being.

The GAP is a habit. It's a habit we can fall into literally hundreds of times per day. We can spend hours each day in the GAP—unhappy, resentful, regretful.

If you spend extended periods of time in the GAP, the compound effect of it will heavily shorten your life span.

Research shows that the rate at which your body ages is modulated largely by how your genes interact with exposure to stressors.

Exposure to short-term stress can actually strengthen your cellular response (i.e., "hormetic stress"). Hormetic stress promotes longevity by activating defense mechanisms in your body.

However, prolonged and extended exposure to stress overwhelms your system, which then has to compensate and overwork (i.e., "toxic stress"), which shortens your lifespan.[2]

Put simply: if you're continually stressed or upset, you're wearing your physical body down. The compound effect of the GAP is monumental. Each time you experience the GAP, it is the equivalent of a microtrauma to your system. Over time, those microtraumas add up, and can eventually break you down.

The reverse of this is also true—being in the GAIN is restorative, healing, and empowering.

Research shows that optimistic people often live 10+ years longer than pessimistic people.[3]

One of my favorite examples is a longitudinal study on happiness that followed a group of 180 Catholic nuns from the School Sisters of Notre Dame.[4] All of them were born before 1917. When they became nuns, they were asked to write autobiographical journal entries.

More than five decades later, researchers coded the entries for positive emotional content. They were wondering if positivity as a 20-year-old could predict how a person's life turned out, and how long they lived.

The nuns whose entries contained overtly joyful content, explicitly describing positive emotions in their descriptions, lived an average of nearly 10 years longer than the nuns whose journal entries were more negative or neutral.

By age 85, *90 percent* of the happiest group of nuns were still alive, compared to only 34 percent of the least happy nuns.

That's a massive difference.

When these nuns were 20 years old, they weren't basing their happiness on how long they thought they'd live. Instead, they lived longer lives because they were happy.

Other research shows that unhappy people get sick easier. For instance, one study showed that unhappy employees take, on average, 15 extra sick days per year.[5]

In another study, subjects were first assessed on their happiness levels, then injected with a strain of cold virus. One week later, those who were happier at the beginning of the study had fought off the virus better than the less happy people. They felt better and had fewer objective symptoms of the virus—meaning they had less sneezing, coughing, inflammation, and congestion.[6]

The way you mentally filter experiences shapes your emotional and physical response to those experiences.

There's an entire field now based on this premise: *epigenetics,* which shows that our perception of events and situations shapes how those events affect us.[7]

Research shows that your interpretation of events, despite their objective characteristics, determines the impact of stress and illness on your body.[8,9]

The way you interpret an experience literally affects how your body metabolizes that experience.

Perception shapes biology.

There are dozens of reputable studies that highlight this fact, but I'll provide two very interesting ones just to prove the point.

The first study found that your belief about the physical activity you're doing impacts the health benefits you get from that activity.[10] In that study, 84 women who cleaned hotel rooms were measured on various health factors, such as weight, BMI (i.e., body mass index), waist-to-hip ratio, blood pressure, etc.

Half of these women were told that their work was "good exercise" and satisfied the Surgeon General's recommendations for an active lifestyle.

Examples of how their work was exercise were provided.

The other half of the women were not given this information. They were just tested on their health factors.

Although the daily behaviors did not change among these 84 women, four weeks after the intervention, the "informed group" perceived themselves to be getting significantly more exercise than before. They were now framing their work as "exercise," which they previously had not done.

Compared with the control group, the "informed" women showed objective decreases in weight, blood pressure, body fat, waist-to-hip ratio, and BMI.

Their bodies changed and they became fitter and healthier.

This was not due to a change in their behavior, because their behavior did not change. This physical change could only be explained by a change in how they *perceived their behavior.*

According to the Harvard researchers who ran this study: "These results support the hypothesis that exercise affects health in part or in whole via the placebo effect."

COMPARISON MAKES YOU UNHAPPY

"Comparison makes you unhappy, and there's no end to comparison in the world, if that's the path you choose."

In the second study, researchers found that your belief about whether a certain food is healthy or not influences how your body digests and reacts to that food.[11]

In the study, participants were split into two separate groups. One group got an "indulgent" milkshake with a label saying it was 620 calories and very high in fat.

The other group got a "sensible" milkshake with a label saying it was 120 calories and filled with nutrients.

Both milkshakes actually contained 380 calories and had the same nutrients.

In order to test the effects of the people's milkshake perception on their actual physical response, the researchers took blood samples from the participants at three different time points.

They were specifically measuring the gut peptide *ghrelin*, which is an essential indicator of energy insufficiency.

When your body has low energy or an empty stomach, ghrelin tells your brain you're hungry and should eat. After you eat, your body suppresses ghrelin levels, which signals to your brain that you're satiated or full.[12]

The full study lasted 90 minutes.

The first "baseline" blood sample was taken after a 20-minute rest period. After the first sample was drawn, the participants were told to view the misleading label of the milkshake they were going to consume.

Their blood was drawn a second time at 60 minutes after the study started. After the second blood draw, they were instructed to consume their milkshake within 10 minutes of their second blood draw.

They then received a third blood draw at 90 minutes, after they had consumed their milkshake.

Those who consumed what they believed to be an "indulgent" 620-calorie milkshake had less ghrelin in their blood after consuming the shake. Their body thought they were full, and they believed it.

Conversely, those who thought they drank the "sensible" 120-calorie milkshake had *more ghrelin* in their blood, which meant their body wasn't feeling full.

When asked how they felt, this group said they didn't feel full.

All participants consumed the same milkshake.

The content wasn't what fundamentally mattered.

Rather, it was the context that shaped the meaning and effect of the content. The context was the view or framing of the experience.

Take, for example, trauma. Two people could experience the same event and one of them codes the experience as "traumatic" while the other person does not.

So much of experience comes down to the meaning or framing a person gives to it.

When you change the context, you change the meaning. The meaning determines the psychological and physical impact of the content.

The most fundamental context for everyone, in every situation, is how they measure the value of their developing experiences as either negative or positive.

Are they in the GAP or the GAIN?

If you're going into the GAP dozens or hundreds of times per day, the psychological and physical impact of that are very real. Being in the GAP has a tangible physical effect—it is heavy, anxious, stressed, unhappy.

The GAIN also has a tangible physical effect—it is light, energizing, freeing, and confidence building.

The GAIN is the most powerful and energizing context for viewing any experience.

Without question, the reason the "happy" nuns lived 10 years longer than "unhappy" nuns isn't because they had fundamentally different lifestyles. Rather, the happy nuns simply perceived or coded the experiences they were having as "positive," whereas the unhappy nuns coded *the same experiences* as negative or neutral.

The difference between viewing an experience as positive or negative is tantamount to viewing a milkshake as 620 calories or 120 calories.

When you're in the GAIN, you perceive everything in your life—even the challenging experiences—as a GAIN.

You could be going through a challenging and even stressful experience, but your body can positively handle that experience because you're framing it as a GAIN.

No one's life is without serious problems, but you still have a choice on how you see them.

Take, for example, my friend Jeff, who recently got divorced. He was not expecting that divorce at all. He was 100 percent committed to his wife and loved her with his whole soul. But she decided she wanted a different lifestyle, one that went fundamentally against the belief and value system they had previously shared.

Jeff spent nearly 18 months trying to change his wife's mind, but it was set. It became clear divorce was the only answer.

Jeff wanted to maintain a positive relationship with his now ex-wife. In order to do so, he had to be intentional about how her framed her specifically and how he framed their past relationship as a whole.

It became clear to Jeff that his wife had gone through a great deal of emotional trauma and confusion leading up to the divorce, which led to her radical shift in beliefs and personality.

Rather than being mad at her for these changes, Jeff decided to have compassion. He could see that she was dealing with serious psychological problems.

He didn't blame her for that.

He didn't blame himself either.

He also wasn't mad at himself for how things turned out. He believed he truly did everything in his power to save his marriage, and that in the end, he couldn't control his wife's shift in beliefs and goals.

It was important to Jeff to stay in the GAIN for a few crucial reasons. He knew that something this serious—getting divorced from a marriage he had for nearly 15 years—could derail him for months, years, or even the rest of his life.

He didn't want that to happen.

Together, they had three young children, and he wanted to minimize the damage as must as possible for those kids.

He had no regrets about his marriage.

He loved his wife.

He was sad it was over. But Jeff was also a highly spiritual person, and chose to believe that God had something different and even better prepared for him.

He only wished good things for the new lifestyle and journey his wife chose for herself.

He was committed to continuing to love her and respect her, not only for the kids' sake, *but because he wanted to love and respect her.*

He chose to view the whole experience as a GAIN.

The 15 years they were married were a grand and beautiful adventure. He wouldn't take that back for the world. They also had three gorgeous kids together, which are the biggest GAINS in his life.

He wasn't mad at his wife because he chose an empathic and intentional framing about why she made the decisions she did.

She was not a "bad person" or a "villain."

He chose to frame her as a beautiful person, one he loved and admired, but one he could no longer be in a marriage relationship with.

To be absolutely clear: this was the most painful experience Jeff has ever been through. But sometimes your hardest experiences can be your most potent peak experiences—which teach you lessons and provide perspectives that truly clarify what you want for yourself.

By staying in the GAIN, Jeff was able to frame his past positively—even with gratitude—and to actively increase his hope about his future.

He wasn't derailed for long.

He didn't go into a slump.

He didn't feel like he went "backward" as a person, but rather that he was continuing to GAIN forward.

Being in the GAIN allowed him to take the stress of this new experience and become healthier and better, not worse.

Being in the GAIN doesn't just make you happier. It makes you more resilient to challenges. It increases your health and longevity.

Given that you now understand the physical and psychological impact of being in the GAP or the GAIN: the remainder of this chapter will break down some basic strategies for catching yourself when you inevitably go into the GAP.

BE UNIQUE, DON'T COMPARE

"Instead of focusing on self-comparison, you focus on valuable thinking and action, created through your unique thoughts and experiences."

You will learn how to quickly get back into the health and wellness of the GAIN.

Stop Comparing and Practice Gratitude

"Comparison is the thief of joy."

—Theodore Roosevelt

The GAP is everywhere, even in my 2-year-old twin girls.

Recently, Zorah wanted to play with our rubber kitchen spoons. I handed her all six. But Phoebe got ahold of one and Zorah became inconsolable.

Zorah began chasing Phoebe, desperately *needing* that one spoon.

She couldn't appreciate the five in her hand that she had previously wanted so badly.

She could see only the one spoon she *didn't* have.

Zorah was in the GAP.

Being in the GAP creates scarcity.

It also stops you from being grateful and generous.

Zorah couldn't enjoy the fact that Phoebe was having fun with that one spoon, nor that she had more spoons than she had hands to hold them.

Zorah could only see what she perceived to be *missing.*

Of course, I understand I'm talking about a 2-year-old, and yes, I understand that in many ways that's not a fair comparison. But ask yourself how many times you take a view on something that is similar to a toddler. When I asked myself that question, I realized it was far more often than I'd like to admit.

We were at Disney World a few days later and ordered some food. The one kids' meal we ordered came with a cookie. My wife, Lauren, split the cookie into four pieces so the kids could share.

After eating his piece, my son complained that his had been the smallest piece.

Straight into the GAP.

The GAP robs you of enjoying your life.

It robs you of appreciating what you already have.

It completely kills the reward of any positive experience you have or progress you make.

Before getting the cookie, it was the only thing my son wanted in that moment. He was obsessing about it, even begging for it. Any amount of cookie would have been amazing.

After he got the cookie, he quickly compared it to something else—the size of the other cookie chunks the other kids were eating.

Not only was he unhappy, *he got zero satisfaction out of his cookie.*

He may as well have not eaten it.

He was actually *worse off* than before he got the cookie.

In both of these situations, being in the GAP stopped Zorah and our son from truly appreciating that their situation had indeed *advanced.*

They had GAINED but didn't see or feel that GAIN because they were swallowed up by the GAP.

They both developed an inflated sense of status from what they believed they deserved.

Zorah was focused on the fact that she had gone from six spoons to five, and couldn't see that she'd actually gone from zero to five, plus Phoebe got one as well.

After being handed six spoons, she believed she *deserved* those six spoons, which made having one taken away a violation of both her status and sense of fairness.[13]

She became emotionally reactive and irrational, failing to appreciate the fact that she had indeed GAINED five spoons.

Instead, she was miserable with her five.

She may as well have had none.

At that point, she was *worse off* emotionally with five than before when she had none.

Our son didn't appreciate that he'd gone from having no cookie to having *some* cookie. He was measuring his experience in a way that made him miserable.

He was in the GAP, feeling he'd been treated unfairly, and bitterly envying the microscopically bigger cookie chunks his siblings were eating.

He wasn't embracing his own GAIN.

He was comparing his experience to another person's experience.

According to research in economic decision-making, if a person feels they've been given an unfair deal, they will often reject the offer entirely, even when doing so leaves them with nothing rather than something.[14,15,16]

Research shows that people with low emotional intelligence are highly sensitive to "fairness violations."[17] They really want everything to be "totally fair" or "weighted in their favor" or they'll be upset—essentially throwing a tantrum to get what they want or trying to prove that they're in control.[18]

They quickly get emotionally attached to what they believe "should be theirs," and if they don't get that, they break down.

They go into the GAP because their "want" becomes a "need."

As with all things, an obvious antidote to emotional reactivity and an unhealthy need for "fairness" *is gratitude.*

Research shows that people who are grateful don't overly obsess over "fairness" or comparisons.

Instead, they can make smart short-term economic decisions that put them ahead even if the outcomes are unequal for all parties involved.[19]

Being grateful helps you appreciate your GAINS.

It also helps you make smart short-term and long-term decisions.

To be clear: being in the GAIN doesn't mean you're a pushover. It doesn't mean you accept unfair treatment.

It simply means you appreciate your GAINS and don't get overly reactive or in the GAP when your situation isn't exactly how you felt it should be.

Rather than getting emotionally reactive and caught up in small moments, you appreciate your GAINS and learn from your experiences.

Time for a quick exercise. Pull out your journal and answer the following questions:

- When was a time you went into the GAP because you went from *wanting* something to believing you *needed* it?
- When was a time you went into the GAP by comparing yourself to someone else?
- When was a time you used gratitude to reframe a situation into a GAIN and move forward?

Call Yourself Out and Give Others Permission to Call You Out

> *"Language is very powerful. Language does not just describe reality. Language creates the reality it describes."*
>
> —Desmond Tutu, South African Anglican theologian and human rights activist

Colleen Bowler founded her financial advising firm, Strategic Wealth Partners, in 1991 in the midst of a divorce and custody battle, and while raising her 3-year-old son.

She qualified for earned income credits her first 2 years in business, making around $14,000 per year.

Every year, she did better and better, growing her business and team. Despite building a highly successful firm over the years, winning numerous awards, and even becoming an associate coach at Strategic Coach, *she never gave herself any credit.*

Every year, she measured herself against the top producer in her area, so she never felt she was actually succeeding.

A big switch happened for Colleen in January of 2004, when one of her team members finally called her out.

Every January, they set new targets for the coming year for what they wanted to accomplish. And after the yearly goal-setting and planning meeting, where the objectives got bigger than the last, one team member who had been there for years said:

> "Why do we never celebrate our successes? Last year we hit all of our numbers and it doesn't seem to even matter. Now we are just focusing on this year and hitting bigger numbers."

Colleen heard what this team member was saying, and as a result, they started having celebration parties every January to celebrate their successes the previous year. The result was immediate. Everyone in the office was much happier. It was tangible.

Around that time, Colleen had gotten mad at her then teenage son about his performance in school. He told her:

> "Mom, you know, it's never good enough. Nothing is ever good enough for you. And the real reason is that you're never good enough for yourself."

That conversation really caused Colleen to reflect deeply about her life. Her son had called her out.

Both Colleen's son and her team were saying the same thing.

She began reflected on why nothing was ever good enough in her life.

She finally gave herself permission to love herself and be happy.

This got her out of her GAP-mindset.

She began celebrating her GAINS much more, and became happier as a result.

Everyone around her became happier too, because she was able to get off the treadmill of relentlessly "needing" the next thing in order to feel worthy. She began to appreciate what she and others accomplished. She became proud of herself and others.

Being in the GAIN didn't stop her from continuing to grow and advance as a person and in her business. Quite the contrary—her growth accelerated once the weight of the GAP was no longer around her neck.

MEASURE YOUR OWN PROGRESS

"Measuring your own personal progress keeps you out of comparison with others."

It's important to have compassion and appreciation for yourself.

You'll be in the GAP from time to time. But now that you have this framework and language, you can call it out when you see it.

On several occasions while i was writing this book, Tucker Max, my editor, would tell me that I had slipped into the GAP. Literally just this morning, I emailed him about my desires for this book and he said, *"AHEM, are you in the GAP or the GAIN?"*

A few weeks ago, I was cleaning out my garage and I went into the GAP big time. Our kids are very industrious and love using tools, building stuff, taking stuff apart, and putting it back together. Our garage sometimes looks like a junkyard.

While I was cleaning the garage, my son poked his head out the door and said, "Looks good, Dad!" in a positive and upbeat tone.

I don't know why, but I took the item in my hand and threw it at the ground. "Why is this garage always messy?!" I grumbled.

He didn't know what to say, so he just quietly closed the door. "Okay, Dad."

The weird part was, before he stuck his head out the door, I wasn't even in a bad mood. I was totally fine. But I went into the GAP as a reaction, or maybe even as a habit.

As I sat there after he left, I wondered:

> *What the heck am I doing? I'm cleaning this garage because I want to. Why did I just go into the GAP? My son was appreciating my progress. He was encouraging and supporting me!*

By going into the GAP, I devalued my own progress and efforts to clean the garage while simultaneously rejecting my son's positive reinforcement.

Rather than being ashamed of going into the GAP, I called my son back out and apologized. I hugged him and thanked him for his kind words.

"I'm sorry I went into the GAP on you," I said.

He thanked me for my apology, and it turned into a great moment. It helped both of us realize the darkness of the GAP. It also helped us stay in the GAIN. The experience actually brought us closer together because my son was able to see me admit when I made a mistake, and he watched me resolve it quickly.

If you go into the GAP on someone, just call yourself out and apologize. Don't make it a big deal. We're all human. Just get out of the GAP and back into the GAIN.

"Whoops, I went into the GAP. Sorry about that."

Now that you have language to describe it, you will see the world differently.

You will see the GAP as it happens.

You'll see it when you turn on the TV.

You'll hear it in conversations.

You'll catch yourself, maybe even in the next 20 minutes, going into the GAP about something.

Now that you have language for *The GAP and The GAIN,* you can use this amazing tool to improve your life.

Start using the GAP and GAIN language in the following ways:

- Call yourself out when you catch yourself in the GAP. Immediately look for and vocalize the GAIN.

- Tell five people you know and love about *The GAP and The GAIN*. If you so choose, get them a copy of this book so they can live more in the GAIN themselves.
- Give those five people permission to call you out when you're in the GAP.
- Help others see and appreciate their own GAINS more by (1) asking them about their recent progress, and (2) pointing out to them their progress. It can be very humbling and empowering to have someone recognize or point out your progress. Be that person who acknowledges other people's GAINS.
- When you're in a difficult situation, help yourself and others find the GAIN. Rather than being upset, you could ask, *"What is the GAIN in this?"* Or *"How can we turn this into a GAIN?"*

Practice Mental Subtraction

"Is there a good way to 'unadapt' to positive events? Perhaps thinking about the absence of those positive events would work."

—Minkyung Koo, Sara Algoe, Timothy Wilson, and Daniel Gilbert[20]

In the 1946 Frank Capra film *It's a Wonderful Life,*[21] an angel named Clarence appears to a man named George Bailey, who is about to jump off a bridge and end his life.

Clarence takes George through a spiritual tour of the world as it would have been had George never been born.

Rather than having George think of all the good things in his life, Clarence allows George to see all the ripples and repercussions that would have occurred if he'd never been born.

George is allowed to see a world devoid of all the good things he had.

By imagining *the absence* of everything good in his life, and the negative impact of him never being born, George realizes just how rare and precious the good things in life actually are.

His outlook on life *instantly* changes.

Borrowing this idea, psychologists have conducted tests to see if thinking of the absence of the good things in your life could make you appreciate them more—a concept called *mental subtraction*.

The results are clear: mental subtraction is one of the most effective science-based techniques for boosting gratitude and happiness.[22]

Indeed, research shows that imagining the absence of a positive event in your life has a more powerful effect on you than simply looking back on that positive event. Likewise, imagining the absence of an important person in your life can be more powerful than simply appreciating the fact that they are in your life.

One study found that mentally subtracting a material possession you've previously enjoyed increases your happiness with that item more than simply thinking back on when you purchased it.[23]

Research also shows that when it comes to romantic relationships, those who imagined never having met their romantic partner reported far higher levels of relationship satisfaction after doing the mental subtraction exercise.[24]

What if right now, you lost your good health?

Or if immediately you could no longer walk?

Or you went blind?

How would any of that feel?

Now think about a very important person in your life.

What if right now, that person died?

Or what if you'd never met that person in the first place?

How different would your life be?

For me, the thought of never having met my wife is simply awful. I am so sad to consider that possibility, and it helps me really appreciate the fact that she is in my life and we have a loving and committed relationship.

Being in the GAIN is appreciating everything in your life, including the progress you've made as a person. It's about measuring yourself against where you were before. It's about seeing everything in your life *as a GAIN*.

One challenge we all face is taking our lives for granted. This is why mental subtraction is so powerful.

By imagining that the important things and people in your life don't exist, you can genuinely start to appreciate what you have.

By imagining that your greatest achievements or progress never occurred, you can see how far you've actually come.

Rather than measuring yourself against arbitrary and changing ideals, you measure yourself in the GAIN, which is what you tangibly have and have experienced in the real world.

Let's take some time to start focusing on the GAINS in your life.

Start by mentally subtracting something important to you. Here are the steps:

1. **Pull out** a piece of paper and a pen.
2. **Select one** specific thing to mentally subtract: it could be a relationship, an achievement, your health, a possession.
3. **Imagine** how your life would be if you never had that one thing, or if it was instantly taken away from you forever.
    a. Picture the impact that would have on you right now.
    b. Think about how losing that one thing would affect your future.
    c. How would it affect others?
4. **Write down** how your life would be different.
5. **Now, refocus** on the present moment and this one thing in your life that you've been focusing on. *This one thing is a huge GAIN in your life.*
    a. How can you appreciate this GAIN more than you have up to this point?
    b. How can you turn this GAIN into even more GAINS?
    c. How have your thoughts and feelings changed about this one thing by doing this exercise?
    d. How do you feel about your life in general right now?

6. Repeat: choose another specific thing, event, possession, achievement, health, or person.

One night while eating dinner as a family, Lauren and I did a thought experiment with our kids, applying mental subtraction.

"What if every time you went into the GAP, we took away the thing you were complaining about?" I asked.

"Complain about skiing; okay, we're done for the day.

"Complain about your iPod; all right, it's gone.

"Complain about what's for dinner; okay, you get none.

"If we took away everything you went into the GAP about, how much would you have?"

"Not much" was their response.

It was a simple thought exercise, but we could tell by the looks on the kids' faces that it was a powerful moment. They're much better these days about being in the GAIN and being grateful.

Think about it for a second: *What if you literally and immediately lost whatever you went into the GAP about?*

You complain about your job: now you've lost it.

You complain about your house: now it's gone.

You get upset that your child made a mistake: now they're gone from your life for good.

This doesn't mean you don't recognize real problems. Or that you stop trying to make things better. It simply means you see the possibility that you could lose the thing you are complaining or frustrated about, and then you understand the emotion that creates in you.

Thankfully, in the real world we don't literally lose the thing we go into the GAP about. *But we do damage it.*

We damage our own experience. And when it comes to other people, we damage them as well.

We all go into the GAP way too much.

We go into the GAP about ourselves, undervaluing and underappreciating ourselves.

We go into the GAP about other people, turning them into a problem or an enemy.

We go into the GAP about far too many things, and perhaps it's a good time to stop complaining.

Will you get out of the GAP?

Give Yourself 5 Minutes in the GAP, Then Move Forward

"One thing that makes it possible to be an optimist is if you have a contingency plan for when all hell breaks loose. There are a lot of things I don't worry about, because I have a plan in place if they do."

—Randy Pausch[25]

From 1984 to 1988, Kim Butler was a college soccer player at Principia College. Given that Principia was a small college, and that women's college soccer was a fairly new concept, the team was made up of several girls who had never even played soccer before.

Because most members of the team were not skilled players, the coach focused on two key metrics:

1. Mindset
2. The ability to run . . . and keep running

For the first several games, this ragtag team got crushed by their opponents. Each time they lost, they were emotionally broken. But their coach had a rule where he allowed them to be down in the dumps for only 5 minutes.

They had 5 minutes to be in the GAP, then they needed to move on.

There were no locker rooms. So after the games, the muddy and sweaty players and coaches would get on the bus and drive the hour or two back to Principia.

The coach would start a timer for 5 minutes.

"Okay, you've got 5 minutes to sulk."

The bus would be dead silent for those 5 minutes as the players were devastated and depressed about getting destroyed in their game.

After his 5-minute timer went off, the coach set a 10-minute timer on his watch. For the next 10 minutes, he had them talk about specific *good things* that happened during the game.

He was helping them focus on the positives.

He solved the GAP problem by going straight to the GAIN.

After the 10-minute timer, the coach then set a 20-minute timer. During the next 20 minutes, he had every player point out a specific good thing another player did during that game.

After the 20-minute timer went off, the coach didn't allow them to talk about that game again. He helped them measure themselves backward. Then, after framing the experience as a GAIN, he let the past go.

No more talk about that game again.

Move forward to the next practice.

During practices, the coach would also give them 5 minutes if they went into a GAP. If one of the players was feeling down, or got hurt, or was in a funk—he'd send them away, give them 5 minutes, and then let them come back when there was evidence that the GAP was gone.

By training these soccer players to stay in the GAIN, and by focusing on the highest-leverage metrics they could control (mindset and endurance), the team started winning.

In fact, during the first half of the year, they lost all their games. During the second half of the year, they won all their games. *And they ended up winning the NCAA Division II Championship that year!*

They literally won the championship with a very simple strategy: they gave themselves 5 minutes in the GAP, and then shifted immediately to the GAIN.

Once they framed their experience as a GAIN, they moved on to the next practice, then the next practice, then the next game.

Ten years later, Kim became a successful entrepreneur, running a financial advising firm. When she learned about the GAP, she realized she had stopped practicing the principle her soccer coach had taught her, which was crucial to her team's success.

As a young entrepreneur, Kim had developed the bad habit of measuring herself against her continually growing ideals.

She realized why she wasn't as happy and successful as she could be.

She wasn't measuring herself backward.

She'd been in the GAP for years.

She started measuring herself backward, in the GAIN, and immediately she became happier, more confident, and more successful.

She now bases her entire approach to financial advising on a GAIN perspective.

Rather than helping her clients focus on a budget or their net worth, both of which are forward measures, she helps them focus on how much they have saved and how much income they are making off their investments, both of which are backward measures.

Kim asks these questions:

- Over the past 90 days, how much money have you saved, which you now have in case of emergency or opportunity?
- Over the past 90 days, how much income have you earned from your investments?

That's measuring backward.

That's focusing on what is actually tangible, and continually increasing your tangible measurables.

Like everyone, Kim still goes into the GAP. But she lets herself go there for only 5 minutes. Then, once the 5 minutes are up, she goes straight into the GAIN.

Only when you're in the GAIN can you move forward.

Being in the GAIN is how you take responsibility for your life and outcomes. You accept where you are, dust yourself off, and move forward with a smile.

In performance psychology, there is a concept known as *implementation intentions,* which is a strategy to plan for the worst—so you can perform your best.[26]

With an implementation intention, you specifically plan for when things will fall apart or go wrong. You plan for obstacles and setbacks. You also pre-plan how you will respond to those obstacles.

For example, if you're on a diet, a great implementation intention would be planning how you will respond if presented with your favorite junk food, or if you're stressed and triggered to binge on sugar.

This is a powerful, simple, and helpful strategy.

YOU'RE 100 PERCENT DISCIPLINED

"You are 100 percent disciplined to your existing set of habits."

Research shows that applying implementation intentions increases your self-control, even when you're in bad environments.[27]

Rather than wearing out your willpower and watching yourself fail, you have a pre-planned response that takes the guesswork out of your decision-making.

When you have a pre-plan for how you'll deal with obstacles, then you won't get thrown off when you're in a situation and tempted to sabotage your goals.

Decision fatigue happens when you're not sure what you're going to do. It's when you're torn between options and, due to your indecisiveness, you often cave to the tempting worse option.[28] Having a pre-plan in place enables you to be intentional, and to avoid the willpower burnout that comes through decision fatigue.

You know what you're going to do. You have a simple plan in place if presented with an option that conflicts with your goals.

You can have a pre-planned response for any situation. You've got to come up with the scenarios and how you will specifically respond.

As an example, let's stay you're trying to overcome a sugar addiction. You can create a pre-planned response for every time you even think about sugar. Maybe the pre-plan is that the moment you think about sugar or get triggered to have sugar, you drop and do 10 push-ups.

In the beginning, you may miss the mark a time or two. But if you apply your pre-planned response, you'll do push-ups rather than eating sugar.

The goal of an implementation intention is that over time, you turn your pre-planned response into a new habit and improved response to old triggers.

The soccer coach's 5-minute rule is a powerful example of an implementation intention at work. Rather than trying to be perfect and planning to never go into the GAP again, the coach knew his players would likely go into the GAP from time to time, especially after a loss.

Rather than planning for ideal future scenarios, the coach had a pre-planned response for when things fell apart. He trained his team so that they knew the plan for getting back into the GAIN.

Remember, the goal isn't to never go into the GAP. Instead, the goal is to get yourself out as soon as you can.

BJ Fogg, a behavior scientist at Stanford University, has a breakthrough method—called Tiny Habits—which is a simple and practical way of applying implementation intentions.[29] All you do is place a new habit you want after a routine that you already have. This is called a "Tiny Habit Recipe." Here are five examples:

- After I compare myself with another person, I will say to myself, "Are you in the GAP or the GAIN?"
- After I feel discouraged, I will list 3 specific GAINS from the last 30 days.
- After someone tells me about a setback, I will say, "What did you GAIN from this experience?"
- After I start my weekly team meeting, I will ask, "What was your biggest GAIN yesterday?"
- After I open my journal, I will immediately write about one GAIN in my life.

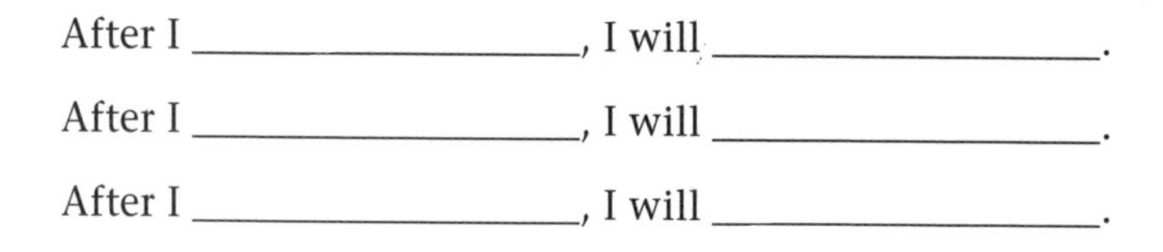

After I ____________________, I will ____________________.

After I ____________________, I will ____________________.

After I ____________________, I will ____________________.

Chapter Takeaways:

- Being in the GAP creates a negative compound effect in your life.
- Being in the GAIN creates a positive compound effect in your life.
- Research shows that happy people often live 10+ years longer than unhappy people.
- How you frame an experience shapes how your body processes that experience.
- Having language for something allows you to perceive it and use it. *The GAP and The GAIN* is a useful tool because there is language for it.
- Call yourself out when you go into the GAP.
- Explain *The GAP and The GAIN* concept to those you love, and give them permission to call you out when you go into the GAP.
- Practice mental subtraction to remind yourself of the GAINS in your life.
- Create a GAIN Tiny Habit Recipe for getting out of the GAP, such as the five-minute rule the women's soccer coach used.

PART 2

GET INTO THE GAIN

CHAPTER 4

ALWAYS MEASURE BACKWARD

Increase Your Hope and Resilience

"You can't connect the dots looking forward; you can only connect them looking backwards."

—STEVE JOBS[1]

Jill could hear the parents choke back their tears as she spoke.

"Last year, Rosie was learning to walk on grass," Jill said.

"Remember how long we were working on that?

"Remember how impossible it seemed?

"I was just reviewing her annual report and was reminded how far she's come.

"I'd actually forgotten about that since she now walks on grass like a champion!"

Phone calls like this have become a routine but essential part of Jill's practice.

They're often emotional.

Jill Bishop is a public school physical therapist who works with kids who have extreme mental and physical disabilities.

Her patient, Rosie, has a rare brain disorder called lissencephaly or "smooth brain." Whole parts of Rosie's brain appear smooth. Doctors have told Jill that children with lissencephaly are incapable of learning and developing.

When she is faced with anything new or unfamiliar, Rosie's screams are high-pitched and deafening. Jill hears a lot of screaming.

Because Rosie's challenges feel never-ending, Jill had entirely *forgotten* that walking on grass was what she and Rosie were diligently working on last year. After months of therapy, Rosie now easily walks on grass and other uneven surfaces. They've moved on to different challenges.

Annual reviews have become humbling and important moments for Jill. By remembering where Rosie had been only a year before, Jill immediately felt extremely proud of her.

She realized that despite what doctors had said, Rosie was indeed capable of more than she was doing. She'd made progress in the past and could continue making progress beyond her current station.

With this deep sense of awe, Jill picks up the phone and calls her client's parents.

Just like Jill, the parents have often forgotten many of the milestones they've previously passed. Given the overwhelming challenges many of these kids face, the day-to-day can be taxing for everyone, especially parents. There's always something to improve or work on.

But if you're not regularly reminded of the GAINS, it's easy to go into the GAP and lose hope.

Tears fall down the faces of these parents as they reflect back on where their child began, and how their child can now do things that once seemed impossible.

Jill believes it's extremely important to be regularly reminded of past GAINS. Without seeing progress, it's all too easy to burn out and give up.

Even the smallest or seemingly most insignificant form of progress, when appreciated, is the fuel these people need to keep going.

"Oh yeah! She can grow! This is working!"

Being reminded that the child *can* grow is the epiphany that both Jill and her client's parents use to maintain hope. Without hope, motivation is shattered.[2] Without hope, you can't have purpose and meaning in what you're doing.

From Jill's standpoint, *progress is everything*. If we're not progressing as people, then we're givingup on ourselves. If we don't believe someone else can make progress, then we've given up on them.

"You can't judge someone else's progress," Jill told me.

In these families, having an internal reference point to determine the right progress *for them* is essential for their happiness and well-being. Otherwise, they're measuring themselves against other families or situations, which can easily lead to GAP-thinking and despair.

Special education teachers regularly burn out and give up.[3] The annual attrition rate for these teachers is an astonishing 13 percent.[4] They leave the classroom twice as much as general educators.[5] The work is often high-stress and low-satisfaction.[6]

YOU'RE ALWAYS GROWING

"You are always growing, and you continually measure yourself in terms of growth."

Jill believes that teachers or therapists of special needs children who primarily focus on "the problems" burn out much quicker than their GAIN-focused counterparts.

Regularly seeing and appreciating progress is key to Jill ability to maintain motivation in her work. Because she takes the GAIN-perspective for each of the children she works with, she discerns progress happening regularly, and she *loves* her job.

When you stay in the GAIN, your motivation to push through challenges is not only enabled but strengthened.

Being in the GAIN helps you discern the progress that others in the GAP would miss.

In psychology, *inattentional blindness* occurs when you are so fixated on one thing that you fail to see everything else going on around you.[7] It's easy to miss the GAINS happening throughout our lives or businesses because we may have tunnel vision on the problem in front of us.

Seeing GAINS gives you hope, confidence, and motivation to keep going—even when progress is difficult or slower than desired.

Your Brain Has Evolved to Forget GAINS

"Human beings are works in progress that mistakenly think they're finished. The person you are right now is as transient, as fleeting, and as temporary as all the people you've ever been."

—Dr. Daniel Gilbert, Harvard psychologist[8]

As humans learn, we quickly adapt to our "new normal," even when that new normal is very different from what our life used to be.

Psychologists call this *automaticity,* and it's how we go from consciously doing something to being able to do it unconsciously.[9]

If you're not recording your GAINS like Jill does for her clients, then you will forget many if not most of your GAINS.

We will now dive into some research on how learning and memory work, so you can see why forgetting your GAINS is so easy.

The *Conscious Competence Learning Model,* generally attributed to William Howell,[10] is a four-stage learning theory that explains the process of automaticity.[11]

Here's a quick breakdown of Howell's four stages. I've included notes from a recent experience fresh on my mind, potty training our twin toddlers:

1. **Stage One—Unconscious Incompetence:** You don't know how to do something and don't even recognize your ignorance.[12] At this stage, you deny the relevance of learning a particular skill. Phoebe and Zorah love getting their diapers changed and expect this process will be a happy part of life until they die. They are blissfully unaware of their own bodily functions.
2. **Stage Two—Conscious Incompetence:** You don't know how to do something but can see your ignorance and lack of skills. You now see the value of GAINING knowledge and skills to address your current deficiency and you begin seeking growth. We strip Phoebe and Zorah down and let them experience their own mess without the security of a diaper. We point out the value of a toilet.

3. **Stage Three—Conscious Competence:** You now know a great deal on the subject and can reliably perform the tasks involved. However, you have to concentrate on the task while doing it. Phoebe and Zorah now become aware when they need to go to the bathroom. "I peed!" is frequently shouted as a celebration. They've learned how to go to the bathroom, but regularly need prompting to remember to take a "potty break."
4. **Stage Four—Unconscious Competence:** You've practiced and performed the task so much that it's become second nature. You can now perform this task effortlessly and unconsciously—even while doing or thinking about something else. Phoebe and Zorah are now "potty trained." They no longer need support using the restroom. It's just a part of life now.

When you get to the fourth stage of the conscious competence learning cycle, you operate in the world differently than your former self did.

You now have new experiences, perspectives, skills, habits, and relationships that influence how you see and behave. You can't simply pretend those new experiences or skills don't exist and go back to seeing things as you did before. They frame your perception and decision-making.

The past, and how we view it, is more a reflection of where we currently are than of the past itself. As the psychologist Dr. Brent Slife states in the book *Time and Psychological Explanation* (emphasis mine):

> "We reinterpret or reconstruct our memory in light of what our mental set is in the present. In this sense, *it is more accurate to say the present causes the meaning of the past, than it is to say that the past causes the meaning of the present*. . . . Our memories are not **stored** and **objective** entities but living parts of ourselves in the present. This is the reason our present moods and future goals so affect our memories."[13]

When you draw on a memory, you always do so from the perspective of your present self.

Psychologists call memory a "reconstruction," because it is always *reconstructed* based on your present views, which influence how you see and perceive past events.[14,15,16]

As Oliver Wendell Holmes, Jr., stated, "A mind that is stretched by a new experience can never go back to its old dimensions."

Why does all of this matter, though?

It matters because without being conscious and intentional, you can easily "forget" or lose sight of your former GAINS.

You can forget what you previously struggled with and overcame.

You can take for granted how far you've come, ignore your progress, and miss out on the confidence of remembering where you were.

This is why it is incredibly powerful and important to keep journals, records, or "annual reviews." Like Jill, you can look back and be *reminded* of the easily forgotten past.

You can be reminded that the "normal life" you're now living may be the dreams—or even beyond the dreams—of your former self.

MOVE TOWARD WHAT'S GROWING

"Your increasing sense of individual uniqueness makes you aware of everything and everyone that's rigidly opposed to any kind of growth. This enables you to identify and move toward everything that's growing."

Going back and appreciating how far you've come keeps you in the GAIN.

By appreciating your GAINS, you more fully appreciate not only where you are now but also your past self. You appreciate everything you've done and overcome.

I've been journaling for well over a decade. I go through about one journal per month. A few years back, I started answering five questions in the front cover of my journals.

These questions allow me to see where I'm at in that moment, what my recent GAINS were, and what I'm trying to accomplish in the short and long term.

I can look in the front cover of my journals and get a snapshot of where I was and what I was focused on.

Here are the five questions:

- Where am I right now?
- What are my wins from the past 90 days?
- What are my desired wins for the next 90 days?
- Where will I be in 12 months?
- Where will I be in 3 years?

It takes me about 5–10 minutes to answer these questions whenever I start a new journal. I answer these questions with about 5–10 bullet points per question.

It's fascinating to open up a journal and spend 2 minutes getting a snapshot of where I was, what my recent wins were, and what I was trying to accomplish at that point in time.

Comparing snapshots of your former self with your current self quickly gets you into the GAIN.

What's startling is that many extraordinary high achievers, even those with many admirers, can feel like failures throughout their careers until they understand the radical difference between the GAP and the GAIN.

For example, new participants in the Strategic Coach program, who have to be earning a minimum of $200,000 to qualify at the entry level, frequently express negative judgments about how they've performed since starting their entrepreneurial careers.

To introduce and teach *The GAP and The GAIN* to new Strategic Coach members, Chad Johnson, one of the associate coaches, takes them through an exercise.

He asks everyone in the group to raise their hands if they consider themselves to be "successful."

As Chad explains: *Almost always, no hands go in the air.*

Despite being obviously externally successful, these entrepreneurs don't feel or consider themselves successful.

On the contrary, many of them actually feel like failures.

They think they're unsuccessful because they're not yet where they want to be.

But the real reason they feel unsuccessful is because of how they measure themselves and their progress.

When no hands are raised, Chad then asks: "What are you going to do to solve this problem?"

After sitting for a while and reflecting the group's, common responses are:

- "Stop setting goals?"
- "Stop trying to achieve something big?"
- "Be positive and sing 'Kumbaya'?"

Finally, Chad writes on the board: **A.M.B.**

ALWAYS.
MEASURE.
BACKWARD.

THE PROBLEM IS HOW YOU MEASURE

"Do you find that no matter how much success you have, you're perpetually dissatisfied with your progress? Does it feel like you're still far from achieving your biggest goals? The problem is not in the quantity or quality of your success and achievements. The problem is how you measure."

Initially, the entrepreneurs don't get what this means.

Chad explains: "There's only one way to measure success. You measure success backward by looking at where you are now compared to where you were before."

It takes a second to sink in.

Chad then asks them to think back on when they started out as entrepreneurs. "How many of you remember when you set the goal: *'If I can make $50,000 in a year, that would be so freaking awesome!'*"

All hands go up.

"Then you pass that milestone and say, *'Oh, if I could make $100,000, that would be amazing.'*"

After helping them see and remember where they came from, and how far they've come, Chad helps them reframe their entire life as a GAIN.

"Look at your team, your current capability, your goals, your lifestyle, your health, and everything else going on in your life. Isn't it amazing, everything you're doing and everything you've created?"

This shift is fundamental and important.

Often, the insight is a bit of a gut punch.

When these entrepreneurs realize how in the GAP they are about themselves and their business, they also realize that they are in the GAP about almost everything in their lives.

They see that they are in the GAP about their team, their spouse, and their kids—because they are measuring them against *where they want them to be*, rather than against where they were before.

They realize they've made happiness an impossible ideal for themselves and everyone around them.

The more you practice measuring yourself backward, the more confident and motivated you will become.

Consider Don Bradley, who emailed me the following after applying *The GAP and The GAIN* principles.

Email subject line: "Don Bradley 2.0"

> "I've been taking the practice you had me do of enumerating my wins for the year, month, and week and I've been applying on the level of the *day*, updating my list a few times a day with my latest GAINS. . . .
>
> "Seeing how much I'm actually getting done in a day is creating this wonderful upward spiral in my self-efficacy: I feel **unstoppable**. Consequently, I get even *more* done. . . .
>
> "This is probably THE greatest efficacy I've experienced *in my life*, and it's coming from pursuing daily goals aligned with my future self and then enumerating my wins during and at the end of each day!"

Being in the GAIN is the most powerful way to measure yourself and your life.

When you're in the GAIN, you see that all of your time is well spent.

Staying in the GAIN enables you to continually use your time better, and create more impactful and meaningful GAINS.

The GAIN allows you to live your life without regrets.

It gives you power over your own progress and experience.

The GAIN creates immediate confidence and momentum.

Don't let your past be forgotten.

Always measure backward.

Now It's Your Turn: Let's Measure Your GAINS!

"The only way to measure the distance you've traveled is by measuring from where you are back to the point where you started."

—Dan Sullivan

Are you the same person you were 10 years ago?

Are your interests and priorities the same?

Harvard psychologist Daniel Gilbert found that when people give themselves time to reflect on their former selves, they realize they're not the exact same person they were 10 years ago.[17,18]

Roughly 15 years ago, when I was 18 years old, I was living at my cousin's house, sleeping on his couch, and playing *World of Warcraft* for 15+ hours per day and sleeping the rest.

I measured success back then by how much progress I made on my character inside the game.

I didn't have a job.

I certainly didn't have a PhD or the six kids I now have.

I wasn't an entrepreneur, nor was I ever intending to be.

I could not have predicted back then where I am now.

Over time, my preferences, perspectives, and goals have changed.

How I measure success has changed.

The same is true for you. You're not the same person you were 10 years ago. You've evolved and improved. You now see things differently than your former self saw them.

You say "No" to things your former self said "Yes" to.

For instance, my former self said "Yes" to playing *World of Warcraft* for 15+ hours per day. My current self says "No" to that, as it would conflict heavily with how I now measure success.

It's time to measure your GAINS.

Pull out your journal. Give yourself some real time on this. Eventually, measuring your GAINS will become a regular practice—something you do even daily.

For now, let's start by going back roughly 10 years.

Where were you 10 years ago?

What were you focused on?

How did you measure success back then?

How has your situation changed?

What do you now know that you didn't know back then?

What have been some of the biggest lessons you've learned over the past 10 years?

What have been some of your biggest accomplishments and achievements since then?

As you're thinking about these questions, it may be easiest to just start with a bullet point list.

Don't overcomplicate this.

The main point is to remember that GAINS aren't just external accomplishments, but *any form of growth or progress.*

These GAINS could include *experiences*—such as vacations or even really challenging events that you've grown through—lessons learned, and relationships built.

However, to maximize the power of this experience, be as specific as possible when it comes to listing your GAINS.

As Dan explains:

> "I've noticed that people who measure their accomplishments in terms of specifics tend to be

happier and a lot more energized than people who speak and think in generalities. Someone who responds to a question like 'How are things going?' with an answer like 'Things are pretty good' isn't actually connecting with their real experience.

"But if you think about specific facts when you assess your situation, this grounds your feeling in reality.

"For example, saying, 'This recently completed project earned ten times as much money as it did last year' is very different from saying, 'This project did pretty well.' If you work in the world of generalities, it's easy to get confused about what's really going on, and your sense of your achievements will be vague and unclear."

Here are some of my specific GAINS over the previous 10 years:

- I married my dream girl, Lauren.
- Together, we adopted three amazing children from the foster system.
- We've also had three other children after years of infertility treatments and prayer.
- I was able to complete my bachelor's in psychology, as well as my master's and PhD in organizational psychology.
- I bet on myself and chased my goal of becoming a professional writer. I've had three major books published, which together have now sold hundreds of thousands of copies.

- I've read hundreds of books over the past 10 years and have upgraded my mindset around money and business.
- I bet on myself and became an entrepreneur and have since built an extraordinary team that supports me and my work—and we truly do help thousands of people improve their lives.
- I've donated over $1,000,000 to my church.
- I'm a better, more empathetic, and more caring person than I was 10 years ago.

That last bullet is a bit general, so to get more specific about "how" I'm more empathetic and caring than I was 10 years ago:

- I'm less reactive to my kids when they're fighting.
- I'm open to my own ignorance and willing to rethink my views.
- I don't judge people who are different from me as "wrong" or "bad."

I could continue this list. But for the sake of this example, I'll stop here.

When people are first introduced to the GAIN, it can sometimes be difficult for them to see or appreciate their GAINS.

Most of us have trained ourselves to brush off compliments and never appreciate our progress.

The more you practice it, the more specific you will get at seeing, appreciating, and framing GAINS.

THE ONLY WAY TO MEASURE

"The only way to measure the distance you've traveled is by measuring from where you are back to the point where you started."

But also, you'll be able to see innumerable GAINS in even the smallest experiences. For instance, you will get to the point where you can list dozens of GAINS in a single day—such as waking up, going on that run with your friend, etc.

For now, start your bullet point list of the biggest GAINS you can think of over the past 10 years.

After you've made your list of GAINS over the past 10 years, let's shrink down the time frame. What about the past 3 years?

Where were you 3 years ago?

What were you focused on at that time?

How were you measuring success 3 years ago?

What do you now know that you didn't know 3 years ago?

How have your "standards" improved?

In other words, what were you saying "Yes" to—in terms of income, relationships, how you spent your time, your habits, etc.—that you now say "No" to?

As you did with the 10-year time frame, make a bullet point list of all your specific GAINS over the past 3 years.

These GAINS include ALL FORMS of progress and growth—tangible accomplishments, experiences, relationships, lessons learned, etc.

Here are some of my specific GAINS over the past 3 years:

- We moved from Clemson, South Carolina, to Orlando, Florida, where we currently live.
- Lauren gave birth to our twins and our son Rex.
- I've invested a lot more time and energy into our older kids. (Getting them into sports and attending their events and matches; taking them on trips; spending meaningful time with them.)

- I finished my PhD
- I bought a second house to be my full-time office for writing and filming (a big step-up from working at home with six kids).
- I published two books: *Personality Isn't Permanent* and *Who Not How.*
- I've tripled my income and become much wiser with money and I began investing consistently in our long-term future.

Now let's zoom in even more.

Make a bulleted list of all your GAINS over the past 12 months.

The British philosopher Alain de Botton said, "Anyone who isn't embarrassed of who they were last year probably isn't learning enough."

To be clear, it is GAP-thinking to be "embarrassed" of your former self. There is no reason to have *any* negative emotions or energy toward your past.

The GAIN enables you to see every experience you've had as a positive.

The truth is, you're not the same person you were in the past. Your former self didn't know what you now know. They weren't as clear as you are now.

Love your former self.

Have empathy, compassion, and respect for them.

They were in a different context than you are now.

They had a different perspective.

They had a different peer group than you now have.

They didn't have the knowledge, tools, or skills you now have.

I share Alain de Botton's quote because it's a good reminder that you should always be outgrowing your former self.

Always make GAINS.

With that said:

- Where were you 12 months ago?
- What were you focused on back then?
- How has your life changed and improved?
- What do you know now that you didn't know back then?
- How has your "measure of success" improved over the past 12 months?
- What are you measuring now that you weren't measuring back then?

Make your bulleted list.

As I drill down to 12 months ago, it's quite amazing how much my own life has changed. Here are some of my GAINS for the past 12 months:

- We've sold hundreds of thousands of copies of *Personality Isn't Permanent* and *Who Not How*.
- My sixth and final child, Rex, was born.
- Lauren and I hired a part-time mother's helper who helps out 20 hours a week.
- Our family saw Mt. Rushmore on a huge family road trip.
- I finally started my YouTube channel, something I wanted to do for around 5 years.

- I launched my high-end coaching program, which added several hundred thousand dollars per year to my business. This new program has evolved me and my entire team, forcing us to up-level our courage, our thinking, and the quality of service we provide to our clients.
- I've let go of many of my unhealthy "needs" and replaced them with much healthier "wants."

Alright, one final time. Let's zoom in again.

- What have been your GAINS over the past 90 days?

Josh Waitzkin, the former chess prodigy and author of *The Art of Learning,* always asks himself this one question every 90 days: "What did I believe 3 months ago that I no longer believe today?"[19]

He uses that question as a journal prompt and truly reflects on it. His goal is to continually be "less wrong."

Waitzkin is in the GAIN.

Adam Grant, the organizational psychologist, Wharton professor, and bestselling author, has spent a lot of time studying what he calls "the joy of being wrong."[20]

In a recent conversation with Dr. Daniel Kahneman, the Nobel Prize–winning psychologist, Grant asked Kahneman how he's handled being "proven wrong" throughout his career.[21]

HOW TO MOVE FORWARD

"Your level of capability in the future depends upon your measurement of achievements in the past. You can't move forward and grow until you've acknowledged how far you've come and have properly measured your GAINS."

"I love it," Kahneman answered.

During that conversation, they discussed Kahneman's blockbuster book *Thinking, Fast and Slow,* based on his Nobel Prize–winning research.[22]

"Do you still agree with everything you wrote in that book?" Grant asked.

"No, I don't, *and I'm so glad.* Because I love learning."

Kahneman is in the GAIN.

Grant is in the GAIN.

Every 90 days, you can change your life. You can upgrade how you think, how you see, and how you live.

You get updates for your iPhone so it can continually function better.

You can also get regular updates to your mindset, your perspectives, and how you measure success.

Pull your journal back out and start listing the GAINS you've made over the previous 90 days. List your tangible accomplishments. But also write about how you've evolved your thinking, your priorities, and your goals.

- What is the most important progress you've made in the past 90 days?
- What lessons have you learned?
- What are you proud of from the past 90 days?

Here are some of my *specific GAINS* from the last 90 days:

- I ended a relationship with my literary agent that had created huge GAINS in my life but no longer made sense.
- I fired my previous publisher and got out of an undesirable book contract.

- I signed a four-book deal with Hay House, the excellent publisher of this book.
- I unwisely invested a lot of money in crypto-currency and abruptly lost half of it. I learned to not invest based on emotion and hype but to stick to a long-term strategy.
- Our middle son went to space camp in Alabama for 5 days.
- We scheduled a family trip next summer to Europe.
- I've been running 5 days per week with the guidance of a running coach.

After you've gone through all of these exercises, you may be thinking that sharing your GAINS is uncomfortable. Many people, including high achievers, do not like sharing their progress with others. This is a by-product of the comparing and competing GAP-culture we live in.

You can always start by keeping your GAINS private in a journal.

However, being in the GAIN is not about boasting or comparison. The goal of the GAIN is to specifically and genuinely measure your own tangible progress, and to help others better measure their own progress as well.

Having supportive and motivating people around you to share your GAINS with is powerful. It's exciting to share your GAINS, and to hear of other people's GAINS, when you're not comparing or competing.

Now that you've practiced measuring your GAINS in this chapter, continue measuring your GAINS on a monthly and even weekly basis. This will dramatically boost your confidence and motivation over time.

In the next chapter, you'll learn how to measure your DAILY GAINS, which will help you stay in the GAIN and maintain massive momentum.

Chapter Takeaways

- It is incredibly easy to forget about your GAINS because your memories are always reconstructed in the present, based on your current perspective.
- Keeping a journal or annual review process is powerful because it allows you to tap back into the context of your former self, and see the massive GAINS.
- Being reminded of the easily forgotten past boosts your hope, motivation, confidence, and resilience.
- You're not the exact same person you were in the past. You've evolved and grown a lot, even in the past 90 days.
- Take time regularly to measure your GAINS for different time frames.
- Always measure backward.

CHAPTER 5

MEASURE 3 WINS DAILY

Maximize the Highest-Leverage Hour of Your Day

"Our eyes only see and our ears only hear what our brain is looking for."

—DAN SULLIVAN

There is one specific hour—the "sweet spot" of your day—that has the biggest impact on both your short-term and long-term success.

What you do during this one hour has effects that far outweigh what you do with the other hours of your day.

It determines how productive and purposeful you are, as well as influences how well your brain functions.

If you use this one hour powerfully, the next 24 will be successful.

If you don't, they'll be wasted.

For most people, ***the last hour of their day*** is a GAP-hour, distracted by media or binge-eating.

THERE'S NO BLAME

"There's no blame to be had for your being in the GAP up to this point. Even if you were raised in a GAIN-minded household, you could easily have picked up GAP-like thinking from the culture that was otherwise around you. After all, measuring backward is counterintuitive to most people."

However, ***the last hour of your day*** can be a GAIN-hour—one that positively transforms how you sleep as well as your entire next day.

What you do during the hour before your bedtime—the "sweet spot"—is critically important.

Your behaviors before bed are coded into your long-term memory.[1] While you're sleeping, your brain processes everything you experienced that day.

But not everything equally.

This is why top-performing athletes—like Michael Phelps, the most winning Olympian of all time—create visualizations of success just before they go to sleep.

Kayla Harrison, the two-time judo Olympic gold medalist, said, "Every night I visualize myself wining the Olympics, standing on top of the podium, hearing the national anthem, watching the American flag go up."

What you do during the hour before bed sets the tone *for the rest of your life.*

This is where your deepest habits are formed.

How you end your day doesn't only determine how well you sleep.

It dictates when you'll wake up.

It orders how clear and directed you are when you awake.

It decides how committed and sold you are on what you'll do and who you'll be the next day.

It defines how effective and alert you'll be the next day.

When you end your day poorly and without a committed plan, you compromise the next 24 hours. Without a clear and committed plan, you become reactive to what's around you and reactive to your own lack of energy.

Reactivity breeds more reactivity.

Research shows that in the hour before bed, 96.9 percent of people use their smartphone, and 90.8 percent *use their smartphones while in bed just before they sleep.*[2,3] Even after they learn that using light-emitting diode screens before bed is terrible for sleep, affects circadian rhythms, and creates daytime sleepiness the next day, research shows that many *people don't care about these harmful effects.*[4,5,6]

Smartphone addiction is pervasive. It leads to sleep procrastination.[7] The scrolling and staring cycle is a dangerous draw on tomorrow's productivity and creativity bank account.

Staring at your phone right before bed is one of the worst things you can do if you want to live an effective, present, and happy life. It has a negative impact on your identity and mindset.

Your identity is how you see yourself, and it drives your behavior.[8,9]

But your behavior also influences your identity.[10] Psychologists have a term, *self-signaling,* and it means that you judge yourself based on your behavior.

If you eat a donut, you'll judge yourself as someone who eats donuts.

If you get up early and go to the gym, you'll judge yourself as someone who gets up early and goes to the gym. Hence, behaviors are self-signaling.

All behavior is addictive.

All behavior seeks more of itself.

If you hop on Facebook and mindlessly scroll, you're more likely to engage in that same behavior in the future.

If you begin investing money in your long-term future, even small amounts, you're more likely to continue that behavior in the future.

HOW TO MAKE JUMPS

"As you move forward, new goals will require you to jump to higher levels of confidence and capability, but you've done that before, time and time again. To remind yourself of this, all you have to do is look back to your various starting points and then to your corresponding achievements."

If you spend the afternoon at a homeless shelter passing out food, you're more likely to continue that behavior.

In a podcast interview with Tim Ferriss, Josh Waitzkin explains the importance of having a "proactive day architecture vs. a reactive day architecture."[11]

What he means by this is: your day can be designed proactively—meaning *by you*—rather than designed reactively—where you're bounced around by distractions.

Your day can be set up so you can live *within* that day in a free and proactive manner, rather than constantly being reactively tossed to and fro by random inputs or external agendas.

In the hour before bed, Josh gives himself time to think about the most important question he's trying to answer or problem he's trying to solve. He then sleeps on it, and the next morning, "pre-input," he meditates and journals about the same question or problem he was thinking about the night before.

Research shows that creativity is primed just following sleep, especially after REM-based quality sleep.[12,13,14,15]

While Waitzkin journals in the morning, he gets flashes of insight and creative breakthroughs.

He's able to tap into the subconscious integration and connections his brain processed and developed while he was sleeping.

As Thomas Edison said, "Never go to bed without a request to your subconscious."

Over the past 5 years, I've experimented with these ideas. Back when I was a PhD student at Clemson University, my evening and morning routine was as follows:

- 30–60 minutes before going to bed, I'd write in my journal for 5–10 minutes. I'd write a to-do list of what I wanted to accomplish the next day. I'd also sketch out ideas for a blog post I'd write the next morning.

- Sleep for 7–8 hours.
- Wake up, hydrate, and immediately leave for the gym—usually around 5 A.M. because the Clemson gym opened at 5:30 A.M.
- Park outside the gym and write in my journal for 10–15 minutes before entering the gym. I'd write about what I was going to accomplish that day, and further sketch out the article I wanted to write that morning. I'd also write my big picture goals and anything else that randomly came to mind.
- Work out for 30–45 minutes while listening to an audiobook.
- Write a blog post for 30–90 minutes before class.
- Class, meetings, and busyness from around 9 A.M. to 3 P.M.
- Go home and han gout with my wife and, at the time, our three foster kids.

By following this routine for 2–3 years, I was able to write hundreds of blog posts in the mornings before class. Those blog posts were read over 100 million times, enabling me to grow a large email list and become a professionally published author before finishing my PhD

I'm a huge believer in planning your day and thinking about what you're trying to accomplish the night before. Then, in the morning, and before you start looking at your phone, give yourself space to meditate and journal about your goals and what you're trying to accomplish.

DON'T COMPARE TODAY

"Don't compare today's value to that of any other day."

Your brain is incredibly powerful just after you wake up.

But if you're not utilizing your "sweet spot" hour, then you won't tap into that power.

By going to bed reactively, you'll wake up reactive as well.

And that's the culturally accepted norm.

The last thing most people do before falling asleep is look at their phone. The first thing most people do upon waking up is look at their phone.

They aren't waking up with a plan.

They haven't primed their brain and subconscious before bed with specific questions to answer or problems to solve.

Instead, they're waking up tired, reactive, and directionless. The rest of their day is spent distracted and reactive.

How do you spend your "sweet spot" hour?

What you're about to learn is the simplest and most powerful evening routine ever.

If you apply this, your days will be far better spent.

You'll sleep better.

Your results will speak for themselves.

Your life will change.

3 Wins Each Day

"Never begin the day until it is finished on paper."

—Jim Rohn[16]

The solution is simple. Start by putting your phone on airplane mode and keeping it away from your body 30 minutes before bed. Ideally 60 minutes before.

Sometime within the hour before going to sleep, pull out your journal.

Research shows that writing down *three things* you're grateful for each day increases your happiness.[17]

Other research shows that gratitude before bed not only makes you feel better but literally makes you sleep better.[18,19]

Writing what you're grateful for is very powerful. But perhaps *even more powerful* is writing down specific "wins" you had that day.

Writing three wins from the day not only boosts your gratitude but simultaneously boosts your confidence.[20]

In his book *Tiny Habits*, the Stanford behavior scientist Dr. BJ Fogg explains that *feeling good* and feeling like you're *making progress* are essential to growth and happiness.[21]

Dan Sullivan has been teaching his entrepreneur clients to write down three "wins" at the end of each day for decades. He even had an app created called WinStreak® where you simply enter three wins each day.

Writing down three wins daily is one of the most effective ways to stay out of the GAP.

You feel like you're *always winning* and making progress. It keeps you in a state of momentum and confidence.

After you've written your three wins for the day, write down the three wins you'd like to accomplish the next day.

No more than three.

Far too many people have 10+ items on their daily to-do list, which is more a sign of being busy than being productive.

The 80/20 principle explains that 80 percent of results come from 20 percent of activities.[22,23]

Rather than having 10 items on your to-do list, have no more than three.

As leadership and business expert Jim Collins said, "If you have more than three priorities, you don't have any."[24]

EACH WIN IS IMPORTANT

"Each win, big or small, is important, and the more you do the activity of identifying your daily wins, the more you'll see greater and greater opportunity for wins."

Make the three wins for tomorrow important wins, not urgent ones.

At the end of each day, Dan writes his three wins for that day and the three biggest wins he'll get for tomorrow.

As he explains:

> "I would go to bed feeling good, but excited about the next day. I would wake up the next morning excited. Then, that day, I'd go out and try to have those three wins. But oftentimes, what would happen is I'd have wins that were bigger than the three I had imagined the night before.
>
> "And then I'd come home and have the same exercise. And what happens out of this exercise—and this has been going on for 15 years with me—is ***I'm always winning.*** . . .
>
> "Regardless of whether there are any setbacks or there's any disappointments, or there's obstacles that I've run into during the day, it doesn't matter. At the end of the day, I have my three wins. Tomorrow I'm going to have three wins. In a week, I'm going to have 21 wins. . . .
>
> "After a while, a couple of things start to happen. First, people start to get very excited. They get very happy. But on the other hand, they realize that it is their saying so that gives meaning to their past and their future. And that's a phenomenal breakthrough to realize, that you're telling the story about your life. The story you've already lived. And the story you're going to live tomorrow. That ability can get stronger and stronger as you go on."[25]

WINNING EVERY DAY

"You'll notice with each winning day—which is every day—that your sense of pride, confidence, and excitement expands and accelerates."

End your day feeling awesome by writing down your three wins. Then write down the three most important wins you can get the next day.

Here are several profound benefits of doing this simple activity every night:

- **Boost gratitude and confidence.** End your day with gratitude and confidence and improve your happiness and sleep.
- **Direct your subconscious while you sleep.** Design your day the night before and enable your brain to "work on it" while you sleep.
- **Give yourself a purpose for the next day.** Plan your day the night before to wake up proactively and with a purpose. If you do not do this, when your alarm goes off in the morning, you'll probably either get sucked back into your phone or just hit the snooze button and fall back asleep.

  A survey of over 2,000 people showed that it takes Americans, on average, *24 minutes to actually get out of bed and start the day*—after two alarms and hitting snooze twice.[26]

  The reason for this is very simple: if you don't know what you're going to do in a given situation, you will default to the most easy and obvious behavior.[27,28] If you haven't pre-planned what you're going to do, then your willpower won't save you from your groggy state. The situation will beat you.[29,30,31]

  Rather than putting yourself in a losing situation, it's better to have made the decision BEFORE the situation arises. You wake up literally every day. It seems like a skill worth mastering.

Make a committed decision and sell yourself on that decision. That's how you avoid losing another willpower battle. You can also set the conditions so it's easier, such as putting your alarm clock across the room with your clothes laid out and ready for you. Michael Jordan summed it up well: "Once I made a decision, I never thought about it again."

- **Retrain your brain to see the GAINS rather than the GAP.** What you focus on expands. By measuring three wins every day, you retrain your brain to start seeing more and more GAINS. Psychology has a term, *selective attention,* that explains that our attention focuses on what matters to us personally.[32,33]

  William James, the Harvard psychologist and father of American psychology, explained selective attention this way: "Millions of items of the outward order are present to my senses which never properly enter into my experience. Why? Because they have no *interest* for me. ***My experience is what I agree to attend to.***"[34]

  Your experience is what you choose to focus on. When you're in the GAP, you're *looking for* the GAP. When you're in the GAIN, you're *looking for* the GAIN. You find whatever you've trained yourself to look for.

Always measure backward.

Measure three wins each day.

Get yourself committed and excited for three wins tomorrow.

WINNING EXPANDS WINNING

"Once you get in the habit of looking for wins, you expand your understanding of what can be a win."

This is the simplest way to retrain your attention and focus.

This is how you get yourself sold the night before on the idea that tomorrow is going to be an extraordinary day.

This is how you go to bed happy and confident.

This is how you wake up energized and with a purpose.

As with all things, you'll get better at seeing the GAINS the more you practice. In the beginning you may still see the GAP all over the place. But day by day, measuring your three wins and then creating three wins for the next day will change how you see the world.

You'll begin seeing GAINS everywhere—even in the smallest of places.

When you find yourself in the GAP, you'll notice it much quicker. Rather than dwelling in negativity for long periods of time, you'll rapidly snap back into the GAIN. To quote the entrepreneur and investor Naval Ravikant:

> "I used to get annoyed about things. Now I always look for the positive side of it. It used to take a rational effort. It used to take a few seconds for me to come up with a positive. Now I can do it sub-second."[35]

You can absolutely get to this point too.

All you've got to do is measure three wins every single day.

Two-Minute Accountability: Report Your GAINS Daily

"When performance is measured, performance improves.
When performance is measured and reported back,
the rate of improvement accelerates."

—Pearson's Law

Measuring your progress is a powerful signal that you're serious about what you're doing.

If you measure your eating, then your eating will likely improve.

If you measure your money—such as spending, saving, and investing—those things will probably improve as well.

Measuring what you're doing is extremely important. Not only does it improve what you're doing by making you conscious, it also proves that something did occur.

As the sociology professor Lyn Craig has said, "What isn't counted, doesn't count."[36]

Record keeping and measuring progress are true principles.

Not only does measurement prove the work got done, but it simultaneously improves motivation and performance.

After writing down your three wins each night, an effective way to tap into Pearson's Law—where you measure and report your progress—is sharing your three wins with an accountability or "success" partner.

It doesn't need to take more than 2 minutes per day.

After your journal session where you've written down your three wins for the day, as well as your three wins for the next day, all you have to do is text what you wrote down to your success partner.

By sharing your wins, you're not actually "reporting" to someone. Rather, you're sharing your success.

There are several benefits to sharing your wins with someone you love and respect:

1. It's energizing to share your GAINS with someone you respect.
2. By sharing your "three wins for tomorrow," you'll feel a sense of accountability to achieve.

3. Humans have a desire to be consistent—thus, by saying you'll accomplish those three, you'll be far more likely to do it.[37]
4. It gamifies your daily progress, making progress into play.

I've personally been doing this for years and it massively improves my focus and productivity—as well as my GAINS.

Every day, my success partner and I send one text to each other.

We report how we did on our wins that day (e.g., 2/3) and then list our three wins for the next day.

That's it.

It's that simple. Keep it simple.

Write down three wins daily.

Create three wins for tomorrow.

If you so choose, include a success partner in your "three daily wins" to increase support, accountability, and motivation.

Chapter Takeaways

- What you do during the 60 minutes before bed has an enormous impact on your sleep quality, as well as the direction and quality of your next day.
- Reactivity begets reactivity. If you're staring at your phone before bed, mindlessly scrolling or consuming, not only will you sleep worse, but you'll continue that same unhealthy addictive behavior the next day.

- To get better sleep, unplug from your phone and put it on airplane mode at least 30–60 minutes before sleep.
- Write in your journal three wins from that day.
- Write down the three biggest wins you'll get the next day. No more than three.
- Do this every day for the rest of your life.
- Pearson's Law states: When performance is measured, performance improves. When performance is measured and reported, the rate of improvement accelerates.
- Having a daily accountability partner combines tracking and reporting. Keep your accountability partnership simple. It shouldn't take more than 2 minutes per day.
- Report your three wins for today and your three wins for tomorrow.

THE WINNING MUSCLE

"When you take the time daily to recognize your achievements, you're building a muscle."

CHAPTER 6

TRANSFORM EVERY EXPERIENCE INTO A GAIN

Take Ownership of Your Past

"Intelligence is the ability to adapt to change."

—ATTRIBUTED TO STEPHEN HAWKING[1]

On September 29, Howard Getson woke up having lost over $2 million before his morning coffee. The 2008 financial crisis had begun.

The stock market continued to crash throughout that day.

Later that afternoon, Howard was at the YMCA doing a workout with his personal trainer. His trainer noticed Howard's complexion and said, "You look pale; is everything okay?"

Howard responded, "Today is the worst day in the market since the Great Depression."

As the words left his own mouth, he realized they were false and he had an epiphany.

"No system works all the time, but there is always something that's working."

It was the worst day in the market FOR HIM, *but not for everybody.*

Trading is a zero-sum game. It wasn't a unanimously bad day in the market—many people lost money, but not everyone did. It was an AMAZING day for some people who were properly allocated or positioned for the specific conditions of that day.

This insight forced Howard to look at his own systems for investing.

The next day, Howard had a conversation with Sean, a trading analyst who worked for him. Howard asked, "If we're so smart, how did we lose so much money?"

Sean replied:

> "We created lots of different trading systems that would have worked yesterday and made money. However, we use a rule that shuts off any system that ever lost more than 20 percent. That rule turned off the system that would have worked great in these conditions."

Back in 2006, Howard had developed a program he called OmniTesting, which tested each of his algorithms on every market and on every timeframe. This process compared the results of those tests using dozens of metrics. If any trading system failed too many of the tests, then that system would be shut off.

WE CREATE MEANING AND VALUE

"Meaning and value aren't given to us. We create our own meaning and value for every experience."

However, one test overrode them all.

If a system ever lost more than 20 percent at any point during their testing period, it would be immediately shut off and scrapped from being one of their active systems because the risk of duplicating that pattern was too high.

Following the major loss, he realized this particular rule of thumb created a generalist trading approach, where everything they invested in would do "okay" in any market condition, but the rule removed specialist trading systems, which could have performed "amazingly" in specific market conditions—like the 2008 crash.

There are different types of market conditions: bull markets, bear markets, choppy markets, consolidating markets, thrusting markets, trending markets, and flat markets.

You can create systems that do very well in specific market conditions (like a bear market), or you can create systems that do okay in any condition. Howard had been going for the "okay in any condition" approach, because he didn't want to lose big.

Unfortunately for Howard, this strategy led him to lose big in 2008.

Although he had lost over $2 million dollars in a single day and was extremely depressed temporarily, with his new insight, he was out of the GAP literally the next day.

He knew where he'd been going wrong in his thinking and investing strategy.

Instead of focusing on creating something that worked in *any* market condition, Howard shifted to having different systems for *every* market condition.

His main focus became developing an overarching system that could identify which trading system to apply and which to turn off as quickly as possible as the market conditions changed.

That insight became the foundation for everything he's been doing since the 2008 crash.

In order to overcome his own subjectivity and biases, Howard has spent the past 13 years focused on trading through artificial intelligence (A.I.). His new A.I. systems removed human fear, greed, and biases. They make smarter decisions faster about which trading systems to turn on and which to turn off as the market conditions fluctuate.

Through the use of A.I. as the tool for switching trading systems to better match the market, Howard is able to increase his likelihood of success in any specific conditions.

Howard was able to take a terrible experience and turn it into a GAIN. First, he used this painful challenge as an opportunity to rethink his assumptions and measurements.

He was able to identify that his measurement criteria were suboptimal. He was able to radically improve what he focused on and measured—which created much better results over time.

Rather than trying to avoid losses as he was before, Howard now measures success by adapting to change.

Taking Ownership of Your Experiences

"Life is simple. Everything happens for you, not to you. Everything happens at exactly the right moment, neither too soon nor too late. You don't have to like it. . . . It's just easier if you do."

—Byron Katie[2]

When you're in the GAIN, you're proactive about your experiences—you look at your experiences and *utilize them* to become more adaptive and successful in your future.

FREE YOURSELF FROM JUSTIFICATION

"When people stop spending their energies on justifying what they want, they free themselves up to focus on creativity and innovation."

Conversely, when you're in the GAP, you're reactive to your experiences—looking at them and being frustrated over what happened. Rather than utilizing your experiences for learning and improvement, you frame them as "a negative."

Whenever you frame an experience in the GAP, you lose power and ownership over that experience.

It's just a "crummy thing" you wish hadn't happened.

Hence, being in the GAP puts you in the passenger seat of your own experiences. You're reactive to whatever happens—and when things don't go how you expected or wanted, then you're the powerless victim.

The GAIN, on the other hand, puts you in the driver's seat of your own life.

You decide what your experiences mean.

You decide how you'll frame them, and you always find ways to utilize your experiences to improve your future—even seemingly terrible experiences are the springboard for amazing clarity and growth.

As Dan explains:

> "Everyone who grows achieves their progress and improvement by transforming frustrating and painful failures into rules and measurements for satisfying success."[3]

The GAP takes away your agency as a person and makes you psychologically rigid.

The GAIN increases your agency and makes you increasingly *psychologically flexible.*[4,5,6,7,8]

Psychological flexibility means that you manage your emotions, they don't manage you. It means you can move forward toward your goals even when setbacks occur. Research shows that low psychological flexibility is associated with the following:

- Higher anxiety
- More depression
- More overall pathology
- Poorer work performance
- Inability to learn
- Substance abuse
- Lower quality of life
- Depression
- Alexithymia (inability to identify and be in touch with your own emotions)
- Anxiety sensitivity
- Long-term disability
- Worry

The more psychologically flexible you are, the less anxious and depressed you will be.

Being psychologically flexible means you can move forward through uncertainty.

It means you control the meaning of your experiences.

When you're in the GAIN, *you become more psychologically flexible.* You take every experience life gives you—difficult or easy, scary or exciting, challenging or accelerating—and you become better as a result.

You're either winning or learning.

For instance, a flexible person may get up for work and find their car has a flat tire. Rather than being upset and paralyzed, they just grab an Uber.

EXPAND OWNERSHIP OVER LIFE

"You use your winning brain to identify, achieve, and measure daily progress, which continually expands your ownership over every area of your life."

Easy.

They'll deal with that flat tire at a different time, but it's not going to bother their day in any way because they have important things to work on.

Alex Banayan is a highly flexible person. In his book *The Third Door,* Alex writes that success is like a nightclub:[9]

> "There's the First Door: the main entrance, where 99 percent of people wait in line, hoping to get in. The Second Door: the VIP entrance, where the billionaires and celebrities slip through. But what no one tells you is that there is always, always . . . the Third Door. It's the entrance where you have to jump out of line, run down the alley, bang on the door a hundred times, crack open the window, sneak through the kitchen—there's always a way."

A fundamental aspect of flexibility is what psychologists call *pathways thinking,* and it's the ability to find or create many workable paths to a given outcome.[10]

The more flexible you are as a person, the more willing you'll be to try *multiple approaches* to getting where you want to go.

The more rigid you are, the more dogmatically you'll try forcing the same approach even when it proves unsuccessful.

As Einstein is credited with saying: "The definition of insanity is doing the same thing over and over again, but expecting different results."

Pathways thinking is a core aspect of *hope.* Research shows that high-hope people take "failures" and use them to adapt and find alternative pathways to their goal.

On the flip side, when low-hope people hit an obstacle, they just disengage and distract themselves—such as by jumping on social media. But they do not learn from their experiences.[11,12,13,14,15]

Rather than being in the GAP and wishing "bad" things didn't happen to you, you take hard experiences and flip them into GAINS.

That's what Howard did during what could have been a debilitating financial loss. He *transformed that experience* into learning and long-term GAINS.

In the book *Peaks and Valleys,* Spencer Johnson, M.D., explains that *the good things in people's lives happen because of what they do during their "valleys,"* whereas the bad things in people's lives happen *because* of what they do during their "peaks."[16]

A peak is when things are going great.

A valley is when things are painful or difficult.

A valley could be a health problem. It could be a financial crisis. It could be losing your job. It could be losing a close friend or a child.

We all go through valleys at various points in our lives.

But again, as Johnson explains: *The good things in our lives happen BECAUSE of what we do in our valleys.*

When you go through a valley, you can learn from that valley or be frustrated by it.

The choice is yours.

Lessons are repeated until they are learned.

If you embrace your valleys and learn from them, you can use what you're going through to create far bigger peaks in your future.

But only if you view those valleys as a GAIN rather than a GAP.

Take, for instance, Richie and Natalie Norton—two people who have been through many deep and dark valleys.

CONTROL YOUR RESPONSE

"Successful people don't control events; they control their response to events."

On the morning of January 7, 2010, Richie and Natalie's three-month-old son, Gavin, died.

They'd been in the hospital waiting and praying for the previous two weeks.

When they found out their son wasn't going to make it, they were both shattered.

"This could ruin us," they said, looking into each other's tear-filled eyes.

They made a decision then and there:

"No matter what happens and no matter how hard it gets, we will live better *for* Gavin.

"We will live better *because* of Gavin.

"We will have a better marriage *for* Gavin.

"We will have a better marriage *because* of Gavin."

This wasn't the only major tragedy they'd endured.

Two and a half years before Gavin died, Natalie's 21-year-old brother, Gavin, whom they named their son after, died unexpectedly in his sleep and without explanation.

Six years after their baby Gavin's death, in 2016, Richie and Natalie lost their three foster children in a failed adoption. They loved those kids as their own and were heartbroken to lose them.

A few months later, Natalie had a stroke that wiped out her memory—thankfully, she's mostly recovered.

In 2017, their 11-year-old son, Lincoln, got hit by a distracted driver while crossing the road near their home. He was in a coma for several days, and they didn't know if he'd survive or if he'd be in a vegetative state if he lived.

It's been one heart-wrenching tragedy after another for the Nortons.

They obviously weren't planning on having any of these experiences.

But as crazy as it may sound, they genuinely believe these experiences have transformed their lives *for the better.*

During hardships like these, Richie used to ask himself questions like:

- "Why did God do this to me?"
- "Why did our child die and so-and-so's child did not?"

He's since come to the realization that there isn't an inherent meaning in things.

Looking for a meaning is fruitless and leads you nowhere.

Looking for a meaning puts you in the GAP because it inevitably leads you to compare your situation with someone else's, creating feelings of either superiority or inadequacy.

Instead of looking for meanings, Richie believes it is on each of us to *create the meanings of the events and experiences in our lives.*

The morning their son Gavin died, Richie and Natalie made a decision: *"We will be better because of this, not bitter because of this."*

From that night forward, Richie changed how he lived his life.

At the time, he was the president of a financial company. After his son died, he quit his job and applied to go back to school to get his MBA. He and Natalie also started writing the book they'd been wanting to write, but had procrastinated about, for the previous decade: *The Power of Starting Something Stupid.*[17]

This terrible experience was a wake-up call for Richie.

He wasn't going to wait on the sidelines to live his dreams anymore.

He now saw that time was very finite, and that no one knew how long they'd be here. Consequently, he vowed to never waste another day of his life again.

He'd never play scared again.

He'd go all out on his dreams.

He would go all-in on his family, and start creating life-changing moments and memories *now.*

As a family, the Nortons have a very unique way of doing things. They live in Hawaii right by the beach. They love walking on the beach, surfing, and relaxing. They regularly go on several-months-long road trips and vacations, and figure out the financial side while they're out on one of their adventures.

Richie regularly takes his boys to the mainland or another country with a one-way flight and an open plan. They go wherever they want and decide at some future point when they want to head home.

Richie's "filter" has become much clearer and finer through his experiences. His filter is his value system, success criteria, and personal rules.

He won't do any business endeavor, no matter how potentially lucrative, if he believes it will take him away from his family.

He won't do anything that isn't on his own timetable, and also ensures pure freedom of location so he can work from wherever he wants in the world.

Richie and Natalie have turned their most painful experiences into extraordinary GAINS.

They are genuinely grateful for their experiences.

VALUE CREATES MEANING

"With increased value comes greater meaning. The things that we value or appreciate the most also have the greatest meaning. Value and meaning in the world, then, are totally created by appreciation."

They've taken ownership of the meaning and framing they give their stories. They aren't reactive about their past, but proactive.

They decide what their past means.

They decide what they'll do as a result.

They're better because of their challenges, not worse.

Don't Compare Your Experiences, Transform Them

"Who controls the past controls the future; who controls the present controls the past."

—George Orwell, *1984*[18]

"Your past is just a story. And once you realize this, it has no power over you."

—Chuck Palahniuk[19]

Years ago, to help his clients increase their learning and GAINS, Dan developed a tool called The Experience Transformer®. The purpose of this tool is to take *any experience* and extract as much value out of that experience as possible.

As Dan explains:

> "One of our greatest abilities as human beings is the ability to learn from our experiences. Humanity as a whole has benefited from those who have analyzed their experiences and derived powerful lessons for all of us to use. . . .
>
> "However, for many people, their lives are all experience and no learning. . . .

> "Even those of us who do try to learn from our experiences can be blindsided by the intense emotions some situations create. We prefer to push these aside until we feel better able to deal with them. However, the opportunity for the greatest learning actually takes place when you feel that intensity. . . .
>
> "*The Experience Transformer* is a thought process that will enable you to quickly transform the intensity of both negative and positive situations into lessons, innovations, and breakthroughs in both your personal and business lives."

To apply *The Experience Transformer*, pull out your journal and follow these instructions:

- Think about any specific experience—positive or negative.
- Ask yourself: What about this experience *worked*?
- What "usefulness" can you get from this experience to improve your future?
- What can you learn from this experience about what you *don't want*?
- Knowing what you know now, because you've had this experience, how will you approach your future differently?
- What about this experience are you grateful for?

When you're in the GAIN, you take full ownership over your own experiences.

By taking full ownership of your experiences and past, you can do whatever you want with them.

You can change what your former experiences mean, and what they don't mean.

When you're in the GAIN, you transform your experiences.

In the GAP, you compare your experiences to other people's, and feel worse off as a result. You don't take ownership of your experiences, but instead, you distance yourself emotionally from them, which ends up creating debilitating trauma of varying degrees.

"Transforming" your experiences means you go back to your former experiences again and again and, through your evolving thinking and reasoning, change what those experiences mean *to you*. You also continually extract new lessons from those experiences.

You view your past *as a goldmine* that you can tap into again and again.

As Dan explains:

> "We're not usually given encouragement to deal with the negative aspects of our experiences, but when you can take a negative experience and learn a lesson from it that you can apply positively to the future, you're transforming the negative experience.
>
> "In my own life, I've found that the more I transform my experiences, the more confident I feel that I'll be able to deal with anything new, negative, or jarring in the future."[20]

The more you transform your experiences into learning and growth, the objectively better your experiences will become.

By continuously learning, you'll be enabled to do what your former self couldn't do. You'll be able to create what your former self couldn't create. You'll be able to have what your former self couldn't have.

As Sterling Sill, the American author, said, "Certainly the most successful lives are those that have the most worthwhile experiences."[21]

Transforming your experiences also allows you to *organize your past* in the most effective way possible.

When you have a disorganized past, you don't really understand your emotions or thoughts, even though they're still impacting you.

A disorganized and nontransformed past is chaotic and confusing. Another word for this is *trauma*.

Trauma happens when your expectations are violated such that you lose your sense of meaning for life and worth as a person.[22] It is a dysfunctional belief about an experience that creates ongoing dysfunction in the present and future.

Trauma occurs when a person is *avoiding* and resenting their past, rather than *approaching* and transforming their past.[23]

Your past is not fixed, but flexible.

Your view of your own past actually evolves over time, even imperceptibly.

For instance, one friend took his whole family to Thailand. Upon reaching their destination, all five kids got violently ill and the entire vacation was spent in the hotel bathroom cleaning up after sick kids. It was a horrid experience for everyone involved, but to hear them talk about it now, they laugh and joke! Over time, they have changed their past into a humorous experience rather than an unpleasant one.

APPRECIATE EVERYTHING IN YOUR WORLD

"Proactive gratitude is about appreciating everything in the world around you. It's not initiated by something special the world first does for you, but rather by something special that you first do for the world."

As the grief expert and psychiatrist Gordon Livingston, M.D., explained:

> "The stories of our lives, far from being fixed narratives, are under constant revision. . . . We are all able to color our past either happy or sad."[24]

The past is nothing more than the meaning you ascribe to it.

Traumatic experiences can be changed. They are not fixed.

Motivation is often broken into one of two categories: approach or avoid.[25]

Being in the GAP leads you to avoid your past. It makes you the victim. It stops you from taking ownership.

Being in the GAIN allows you to transform your experiences into GAINS, and give them the meanings you choose.

The sooner you frame your experience as a GAIN rather than a GAP, the faster you'll be able to move forward and heal traumas.

This is actually how you know someone has healed from trauma: they genuinely view their past experiences *as a GAIN.*

They can honestly say they're *grateful for the lessons they learned from them.*[26,27,28]

They're no longer "incapable" or "worse off" because of any experience they've had.

The GAIN is the most empowering context for viewing any experience.

Being in the GAIN empowers you and gives you full ownership over your experiences and past.

Post-traumatic growth occurs as you proactively find benefits from former hardships. You also actively frame tragedies or challenges in a way that gives you greater strength and empowerment than you had *before the experience.*[29]

You can't have post-traumatic growth until you actively transform the experience that hurt you.

In order to experience post-traumatic growth, you've got to actively think about the experience and its aftermath, just as Dan does with his *Experience Transformer* exercise.[30]

You "grow" from the experience by getting "value" and "usefulness" out of the experience.

When you're in the GAP, you don't see any usefulness in certain experiences. Instead, you simply wish they hadn't happened.

The GAP is passive.

The GAIN is active.

When you're in the GAIN, you extract uses, lessons, and purposes from your experience. You become better, more informed, and more capable because of your experiences. You derive purpose and meaning from your experiences.

This is why being in the GAIN is so important.

When you're in the GAIN, you immediately turn hard experiences into enhanced growth, meaning, and purpose.

Taking time to sit down and think about your experiences is what psychologists call *deliberate rumination.*[31] It's where you:

- Actively think about an experience.
- Proactively create the meaning you want that experience to have for you.
- Revise your life narrative in a positive way as a result.

You frame the experience as a GAIN so you can move forward powerfully.

PROACTIVE GRATITUDE CREATES GROWTH

"Proactive gratitude allows you to enter into a special relationship with the world—one that continually grows in value, meaning, and happiness."

This active thinking process is dramatically enhanced when it's done in written autobiographical form—such as in a journal.[32]

While writing about your experiences, include gratitude, which exponentially boosts the effects.[33,34]

When you don't take the time to transform your experiences into growth and purpose—but instead avoid your experiences in the GAP—then you experience what's called *intrusive rumination.*

This is where uncomfortable thoughts and emotions randomly hit you, triggering the painful emotions of the past.

Those uncomfortable emotions and disorganized thoughts are still there because you haven't transformed the experience and chosen what it means.

When you're in the GAIN, you own your experiences.

When you're in the GAIN, you actively transform your past.

You go back to previous experiences and transform them again and again, getting new lessons and insights.

When you're in the GAIN, you become better because of challenging experiences.

You become *antifragile.*

As Dr. Nassim Taleb explains, "Antifragility is beyond resilience or robustness. The resilient resists shocks and stays the same; the antifragile gets better."[35]

If you're measuring in such a way that every day you have an increasing sense of either winning or learning—never losing—it makes you antifragile.

Seeing every experience as a GAIN makes you antifragile.

Turning every experience—even your hardest—into a GAIN makes you antifragile.

Being in the GAIN increases your flexibility *every time you do it.*

Being in the GAIN enables you to continually move forward, regardless of what happened. Not just move forward—but do so in a more informed, grateful, and enhanced way.

Chapter Takeaways

- Being in the GAIN is not simply about seeing life on the bright side. Being in the GAIN is about taking every experience life throws at you and transforming it to serve you.
- When you're in the GAP, you ask yourself, *"Why did this happen?"* and act as a victim.
- When you're in the GAIN, you control the meaning of your past. You cherish your past and use it as precious feedback for clarifying what you truly want and value.
- Being in the GAIN is an approach-motivated way of life, and it enables you to turn every valley into a future peak.
- Being in the GAIN empowers you to take any experience and be better, not bitter.

CONCLUSION

Life, Liberty, and the Expansion of Happiness

"There is nothing noble in being superior to your fellow man; true nobility is being superior to your former self."

—Ernest Hemingway

Thomas Jefferson's formula of "Life, Liberty, and ***the Pursuit of happiness***" makes happiness an unachievable ideal.

Jefferson wasn't wrong in having ideals.

He *was* wrong, however, in *measuring his happiness* against his ideals.

When you're *pursuing* happiness, then you're measuring yourself against whatever you're pursuing.

No one, not even Jefferson himself, could achieve happiness with the "pursuit of happiness" formula. It is an absolutely terrible formula for happiness.

The fundamental basis is wrong: happiness is not something *you pursue.*

The reason is simple: ideals are not something you ever actually achieve. Trying to achieve an ideal *always* puts you in the GAP.

Ideals are like a horizon in the desert. They illuminate the path up ahead, and give you direction for setting achievable and measurable targets. But like the horizon, *the ideal itself is immeasurable, unreachable, and constantly moving.*

Ideals are not for measuring yourself against. Why measure yourself against something you can never reach?

Rather than measuring yourself against an ideal, as Jefferson subscribed, there is a much better formula for happiness, confidence, and success: ***always measure backward***.

"Measuring backward" means you measure your progress based on where you were before.

By measuring yourself backward, you get the following benefits:

- You *liberate* yourself from the GAP.
- You get off the hedonic treadmill of working harder and harder to reach an unreachable target.
- You stop comparing yourself and competing with anyone else.
- You appreciate where you truly are.
- You appreciate your progress.
- You appreciate everything in your life.
- You see every experience as a GAIN.
- You're enabled to transform every experience *into* a GAIN.
- You never start from scratch again, but always with the momentum of all your GAINS behind you.
- You start each new day ALREADY HAPPY based on the happiness you've achieved to this point, and you EXPAND that happiness every day because you know happiness is created by measuring your progress backward.

Today marks the end of ever again pursuing happiness. You're now liberated from measuring yourself against ideals.

Right now, you can make the choice to be happy. This very instant, as you read these words: you can choose to be happy.

You can be liberated from trying to eke out happiness wherever you can find it.

You can be liberated from wishing your life was different.

You can be liberated from a nontransformed past. You have the ability to take any experience you've had and transform it into a GAIN.

You have the ability to take any experience you're currently having and appreciate that moment AS A GAIN, rather than measuring that situation against an ideal.

Every day you measure the GAIN, you're happier than you were yesterday.

You're further than you were yesterday.

You're freer than you were yesterday.

You're more yourself than you were yesterday.

Every day you measure the GAIN, you increasingly see the GAINS in others. Rather than measuring others against unreachable ideals as you have in the past, you only measure their GAINS.

How you see anything is how you see everything.

You train your brain what to see.

The more you measure GAINS, the more you'll see GAINS.

The more you see GAINS, the more GAINS you'll create.

The more GAINS you create, the happier and freer you'll be.

Happiness is your *starting point,* which you expand every time you create GAINS and measure your progress backward.

HOW FAR WILL YOU GO?

"Trust me when I say that one day it's going to hit you—that you woke up happy, that you're smiling for no reason, that your hands aren't shaking anymore. One day, you're going to remember what it was like to be you a year ago, or three years ago, or even a week ago, and you're going to be so glad that you fought. You're going to be so glad that you kept going."

—Bianca Sparacino, Popular blogger[1]

You've *already* made incredible GAINS in your life.

You're so much further along than you even realize.

If you've begun to truly fathom the power of being in the GAIN, you'll immediately be humbled. There will be a moment when it hits you just how far you've already come.

You'll be overwhelmed by your GAINS.

You'll be shocked at all the low moments you passed through.

You'll shake your head at all the miracles and lucky breaks that seemed to go your way.

You won't even know what to say to all the people who loved you and sacrificed so much of themselves to even give you a chance.

I had that moment just yesterday, while visiting my family and being back in the home I grew up in.

I had memories of who I was in the past, and the challenges and obstacles I've overcome to get where I'm at.

I thought back on when I got back from my church mission trip in 2010 and started community college with zero college credits.

I thought about before that, when I was a scared 10-year-old boy hearing my parents fight, and I came home to find my crying dad say, "She's gone, Ben. And she's not coming back."

I thought about feeling completely lost and alone as my depressed father became a drug addict, and as I watched my whole world crumble around me.

I thought back to the thousands of hours I spent escaping life in *World of Warcraft,* living on my cousin's couch, and trying as hard as I could to give up on myself like I felt life had given up on me.

I thought about when I started running, and how I actually watched myself succeed at something for the first time in my life. I remember finishing that first half-marathon, and having my mom and Barker there at the finish line waiting for me. Then I remember completing that first marathon, and being so exhausted I couldn't move.

I thought about leaving on that church mission trip, and committing in my heart that this would be my point-of-no-return experience—and that from here forward, Benjamin Hardy is going to live his best life.

I thought about the hundreds of journals I've filled out and the thousands of books I've read.

I thought about being rejected three times for the job I wanted as a missionary trainer.

I thought about eventually getting that job and pouring my soul into helping those missionaries.

I thought about being rejected by 15 schools the first time I applied to graduate school—then finding the best mentor I ever could, and having him teach me how to write with confidence.

I thought about getting into Clemson for my PhD program, and almost getting kicked out multiple times both for mistakes I made and also because I never fit the mold.

I thought about Bob Sinclair, the chair of the department, who was my lifeline when I was about to be kicked out for good. He was my last chance at finishing my PhD after I'd invested the previous 8 years in college trying to reach that point and almost having it all taken away from me.

I thought about all the fertility treatments my wife endured as we tried to get pregnant for more than 6 years. I remember her putting huge needles in her body and tracking her period every night for years and getting the same result over and over.

I thought about the foster system that hated us and tried illegally on multiple occasions to take our kids away from us. I remembered our attorney, Dale Dove, a God-fearing man who had dedicated his life to understanding the law, who made the other attorneys look like fools. He helped change the law in the state of South Carolina so foster parents could have more rights.

I remember hearing that judge say: "By the court of law, these kids are now yours."

I remember it hitting me that after 3 years of fighting the foster care system in court, and after 3 years of overcoming my own insecurities as a father, I was now actually a father.

I remember defending my dissertation and making all sorts of mistakes, and Bob encouraging me even when I began to doubt myself.

I remember getting that first book deal, and investing all of it into making the book a success. I remember spending far too much money trying to hit the bestseller list and not making it, and feeling like a fraud to my wife.

I remember all the late nights trying to hit deadlines, and often getting sick due to the stress and fear that maybe I wouldn't be able to write the book.

I remember my first product launch, when literally no one bought it.

I remember the first time my launch went really well, and I all of a sudden had way more money than I knew what to do with. And then squandering most of that money because I really didn't know what to do with it.

I remember seeing my wife give birth to our twin girls and later to our little boy, Rex.

I remember all the highs and lows that got me to where I'm at, and I sit here humbled and amazed by the life God has given me.

I'm humbled that I chose to continue fighting, when there were a million reasons to stop at a million previous mile markers behind me.

When I step back and think about it, I almost can't believe it.

Did I really make it this far?

Wow. If I've come this far, and if I'm really living the life I'm now living, then what else could I possibly do?

Life becomes a continual upward spiral.

I've got lots of GAINS behind me. But I have infinitely more GAINS ahead of me, and every step I take forward, I'm further and wiser than my former self.

Increasingly, my clarity of what I want crystalizes and I'm empowered to get it faster than I previously could.

As Dan explains:

> "You'll notice as you go forward that everything you want in your future has the qualities of being both more achievable and more measurable than things you did in the past."[2]

This is what being in the GAIN looks and feels like.

You can have it right now.

You can have it this instant.

Happiness is right here, right in front of you.

The question is: Will you choose it?

Or will you continue measuring yourself against fluctuating ideals and externals?

If you choose the life of the GAIN, then you'll be more humbled and clearer than ever before. You'll make happiness your starting point, which you *expand* every day of your life.

The question you must now ask yourself is: *How far will I go?*

You're the only person who can answer that question.

You're the only person who sets the standards for yourself.

You're the only person who determines your direction.

You're the only person whose judgments matter about your experiences—and your GAINS.

You get to decide how much you'll embrace the GAIN.

You get to decide how many GAINS you'll create.

The more GAINS you create, the more specific and selective you'll become about the life you'll live and the future you'll create.

The more GAINS you create, the more you and your life will become unique and incomparable to anyone else.

No one can replicate you when you're in the GAIN, because no one has the same experiences you're having—and no one can transform your experiences into GAINS the way you do.

You've already made it this far.

Look back at where you were when you started.

What are you going to do now?

How far are you going to go?

You get to decide that.

And with every step you take forward, you get to measure backward and become increasingly humbled at how far you've come.

ENDNOTES

Introduction

1. Jefferson, Thomas. (1763). From Thomas Jefferson to John Page, 15 July 1763. Founders Archives. https://founders.archives.gov/documents/Jefferson/01-01-02-0004

2. National Science Foundation. (2020). *COVID Response Tracking Study*. University of Chicago. Retrieved on March 27, 2021, at https://www.norc.org/Research/Projects/Pages/covid-response-tracking-study.aspx

3. Erez, M., & Earley, P. C. (1993). *Culture, self-identity, and work*. Oxford University Press on Demand.

4. Barnard, J. W. (2008). Narcissism, over-optimism, fear, anger, and depression: The interior lives of corporate leaders. *University of Cincinnati Law Review, 77*, 405.

5. Cubbon, L., Darga, K., Wisnesky, U. D., Dennett, L., & Guptill, C. (2020). Depression among entrepreneurs: A scoping review. *Small Business Economics*, 1–25.

6. McKeown, G. (2021). *Effortless: Make it easier to do what matters most*. Currency.

7. Sheldon, K. M., & Lyubomirsky, S. (2012). The challenge of staying happier: Testing the hedonic adaptation prevention model. *Personality and Social Psychology Bulletin*, 38(5), 670–680.

8. Lyubomirsky, S. (2011). *Hedonic adaptation to positive and negative experiences*. Oxford University Press.

9. Eysenck, M. W. (1994). *Happiness: Facts and myths*. Psychology Press.

10. Grover, Tim. (2021). *Winning: The unforgiving race to greatness* (Tim Grover Winning Series). Scribner.

11. Sullivan, D. (2019). *Always be the buyer: Attracting other people's highest commitment to your biggest and best standards*. The Strategic Coach Inc.

12. Godin, S. (2015). *Poke the box: When was the last time you did something for the first time?* Penguin.

13. Godin, S. (2012). *The Icarus deception: how high will you fly?* Penguin.
14. Campbell, J. (2008). *The hero with a thousand faces* (The collected works of Joseph Campbell). New World Library.

Chapter 1

1. Jansen, Dan. (2020). Dr. Jim Loehr on mental toughness, energy management, the power of journaling, and Olympic gold medals (#490). *The Tim Ferriss Show.* Retrieved March 2, 2021, at https://tim.blog/2020/12/28/jim-loehr-2/
2. Walsh, L. C., Boehm, J. K., & Lyubomirsky, S. (2018). Does happiness promote career success? Revisiting the evidence. *Journal of Career Assessment, 26*(2), 199–219.
3. Fredrickson, B. L. (2004). The broaden-and-build theory of positive emotions. *Philosophical Transactions of the Royal Society of London, Series B: Biological Sciences, 359*(1449), 1367–1377.
4. Park, G. (2021). The benefit of gratitude: trait gratitude is associated with effective economic decision-making in the ultimatum game. *Frontiers in Psychology, 12*, 590132.
5. Sitzmann, T., & Yeo, G. (2013). A meta-analytic investigation of the within-person self-efficacy domain: Is self-efficacy a product of past performance or a driver of future performance? *Personnel Psychology, 66*(3), 531–568.
6. Ravikant, N. (2016). Naval Ravikant on happiness hacks and the 5 chimps theory (#136). *The Tim Ferriss Show.* Retrieved on March 29, 2021, at https://tim.blog/naval-ravikant-on-the-tim-ferriss-show-transcript/
7. Rollings, Michaela. (2014). The difference between wanting someone and needing them. *Thought Catalog.* Retrieved on May 22, 2021, at https://thoughtcatalog.com/michaela-rollings/2014/05/the-difference-between-wanting-someone-and-needing-them/
8. Undisputed. (2021). Shannon reacts to Trevor Lawrence's response to perceived lack of motivation | NFL | UNDISPUTED. FOX SPORTS. Retrieved on July 8, 2021, at https://www.youtube.com/watch?v=MdBIR-NbAjc&t=22s
9. Lawrence, Trevor. (2021). Twitter response to media about his *Sports Illustrated* comments. Retrieved on May 22, 2021, at https://twitter.com/Trevorlawrencee/status/1383467135410655235
10. Lawrence, Trevor. (2021). Stephen A.'s 1-on-1 interview with Trevor Lawrence before the 2021 NFL Draft | First Take.

YouTube: ESPN channel. Retrieved on May 22, 2021, at https://www.youtube.com/watch?v=CjKBGp9Zrko&t=49s

11. Vallerand, R. J., Salvy, S. J., Mageau, G. A., Elliot, A. J., Denis, P. L., Grouzet, F. M., & Blanchard, C. (2007). On the role of passion in performance. *Journal of Personality, 75*(3), 505–534.

12. Bonneville-Roussy, A., Lavigne, G. L., & Vallerand, R. J. (2011). When passion leads to excellence: The case of musicians. *Psychology of Music, 39*(1), 123–138.

13. Vallerand, R. J. (2010). On passion for life activities: The dualistic model of passion. *In Advances in experimental social psychology* (Vol. 42, pp. 97–193). Academic Press.

14. St-Louis, A. C., Verner-Filion, J., Bergeron, C. M., & Vallerand, R. J. (2018). Passion and mindfulness: Accessing adaptive self-processes. *The Journal of Positive Psychology, 13*(2), 155–164.

15. Amemiya, R., & Sakairi, Y. (2019). The effects of passion and mindfulness on the intrinsic motivation of Japanese athletes. *Personality and Individual Differences, 142*, 132–138.

16. Carpentier, J., Mageau, G. A., & Vallerand, R. J. (2012). Ruminations and flow: Why do people with a more harmonious passion experience higher well-being? *Journal of Happiness Studies, 13*(3), 501–518.

17. Stenseng, F., & Dalskau, L. H. (2010). Passion, self-esteem, and the role of comparative performance evaluation. *Journal of Sport and Exercise Psychology, 32*(6), 881–894.

18. Carpentier, J., Mageau, G. A., & Vallerand, R. J. (2012). Ruminations and flow: Why do people with a more harmonious passion experience higher well-being? *Journal of Happiness Studies, 13*(3), 501–518.

19. Rheinberg, F., & Engeser, S. (2018). Intrinsic motivation and flow. In *Motivation and Action* (pp. 579–622). Springer.

20. Keller, J., & Bless, H. (2008). Flow and regulatory compatibility: An experimental approach to the flow model of intrinsic motivation. *Personality and Social Psychology Bulletin, 34*(2), 196–209.

21. Seifert, T., & Hedderson, C. (2010). Intrinsic motivation and flow in skateboarding: An ethnographic study. *Journal of Happiness Studies, 11*(3), 277–292.

22. Duckworth, A. L., Peterson, C., Matthews, M. D., & Kelly, D. R. (2007). Grit: Perseverance and passion for long-term goals. *Journal of Personality and Social Psychology, 92*(6), 1087.

23. Verner-Filion, J., Schellenberg, B. J., Holding, A. C., & Koestner, R. (2020). Passion and grit in the pursuit of long-term personal goals in college students. *Learning and Individual Differences, 83*, 101939.

24. Zhao, Y., Niu, G., Hou, H., Zeng, G., Xu, L., Peng, K., & Yu, F. (2018). From growth mindset to grit in Chinese schools: The mediating roles of learning motivations. *Frontiers in Psychology, 9,* 2007.
25. Shinn, F. S. (2012). *The new game of life and how to play it.* Simon and Schuster.
26. Fromm, E. (1994). *Escape from freedom.* Macmillan.
27. Bay, C. (1970). *The structure of freedom.* Stanford University Press.
28. Veenhoven, R. (2000). Freedom and happiness: A comparative study in forty-four nations in the early 1990s. In *Culture and subjective well-being,* (pp. 257–288). MIT Press.
29. Okulicz-Kozaryn, A. (2014). "Freedom from" and "freedom to" across countries. *Social Indicators Research, 118*(3), 1009–1029.
30. Maslow, A. H. (1943). A theory of human motivation. *Psychological Review, 50*(4), 370.

Chapter 2

1. Godin, S. (2012). *Stop stealing dreams (What is school for?).* Seth Godin.
2. Robinson, K., & Lee, J. R. (2011). *Out of our minds.* Tantor Media, Inc.
3. Robinson, K. (2006). *Do schools kill creativity?* TED Talk.
4. Zalta, E. N., Nodelman, U., Allen, C., & Anderson, R. L. (2005). *Stanford encyclopedia of philosophy.* Palo Alto CA: Stanford University.
5. Ryan, R. M., & Deci, E. L. (2019). Brick by brick: The origins, development, and future of self-determination theory. In *Advances in motivation science* (Vol. 6, pp. 111–156). Elsevier.
6. Fogg, B. J. (2009). Creating persuasive technologies: an eight-step design process. In *Proceedings of the 4th international conference on persuasive technology* (paper 44).
7. Al-Menayes, J. (2016). The fear of missing out scale: Validation of the Arabic version and correlation with social media addiction. *International Journal of Applied Psychology, 6*(2), 41-46.
8. Rhodes, L., Orlowski, J. (2020). *The social dilemma.* Netflix Original Documentary.
9. Ziglar, Zig. (2015). *Master successful personal habits: success legacy library.* Gildan Media.
10. Jan, M., Soomro, S., & Ahmad, N. (2017). Impact of social media on self-esteem. *European Scientific Journal, 13*(23), 329-341.

11. Vogel, E. A., Rose, J. P., Roberts, L. R., & Eckles, K. (2014). Social comparison, social media, and self-esteem. *Psychology of Popular Media Culture, 3*(4), 206.
12. Lin, L. Y., Sidani, J. E., Shensa, A., Radovic, A., Miller, E., Colditz, J. B., Hoffman, B. L., Giles, L. M., & Primack, B. A. (2016). Association between social media use and depression among US young adults. *Depression and Anxiety, 33*(4), 323–331.
13. Kim, M. H., Min, S., Ahn, J. S., An, C., & Lee, J. (2019). Association between high adolescent smartphone use and academic impairment, conflicts with family members or friends, and suicide attempts. *PloS One,* 14(7), e0219831.
14. McCoy, Sandi (2020). How to measure success. Instagram post. @Vsg_queendiet. Retrieved on May 24, 2021, at https://www.instagram.com/p/B-QMbNknkzu/
15. Baer, D. (2013). How Arianna Huffington networks without networking. *Fast Company.* Retrieved on June 3, 2021, at https://www.fastcompany.com/3018307/how-arianna-huffington-networks-without-networking
16. Jackson, D. (1999). I know I'm being successful when. *I Love Marketing.* Retrieved on April 15, 2021, at https://ilovemarketing.com/i-know-im-being-successful-when/
17. Gilbert, D. (2014). *The psychology of your future self.* TED talk.
18. Seneca, L. A. (2004). *On the shortness of life* (Vol. 1 of Penguin Great Idea series). Penguin UK.
19. Sivers, D. (2009). *No yes. Either HELL YEAH! or no.* Retrieved on June 3, 2021, at https://sive.rs/hellyeah

Chapter 3

1. Carey, N. (2012). *The epigenetics revolution: How modern biology is rewriting our understanding of genetics, disease, and inheritance.* Columbia University Press.
2. Epel, E. S., & Lithgow, G. J. (2014). Stress biology and aging mechanisms: Toward understanding the deep connection between adaptation to stress and longevity. *Journals of Gerontology Series A: Biomedical Sciences and Medical Sciences, 69*(Suppl. 1), S10–S16.
3. Seligman, M. E. (2004). *Authentic happiness: Using the new positive psychology to realize your potential for lasting fulfillment.* Simon and Schuster.
4. Danner, D. D., Snowdon, D. A., & Friesen, W. V. (2001). Positive emotions in early life and longevity: Findings from the nun study. *Journal of Personality and Social Psychology, 80*(5), 804–813.

5. Gallup-Healthways Well-Being Index (2008). As referenced in: Associated Press. (June 18, 2008). Poll: Unhappy workers take more sick days.
6. Cohen, S., Doyle, W. J., Turner, R. B., Alper, C. M., & Skoner, D. P. (2003). Emotional style and susceptibility to the common cold. *Psychosomatic Medicine, 65*(4), 652-657.
7. Bhadra, U. (2017). The human perception, cognition, and related epigenetics. *Gerontology & Geriatrics: Research, 3*(1), 1030.
8. Park, C. L., & Helgeson, V. S. (2006). Introduction to the special section: Growth following highly stressful life events—current status and future directions. *Journal of Consulting and Clinical Psychology, 74*, 791–796.
9. Moskalev, A., Aliper, A., Smit-McBride, Z., Buzdin, A., & Zhavoronkov, A. (2014). Genetics and epigenetics of aging and longevity. *Cell Cycle, 13*(7), 1063-1077.
10. Crum, A. J., & Langer, E. J. (2007). Mind-set matters: Exercise and the placebo effect. *Psychological Science, 18*(2), 165–171.
11. Crum, A. J., Corbin, W. R., Brownell, K. D., & Salovey, P. (2011). Mind over milkshakes: Mindsets, not just nutrients, determine ghrelin response. *Health Psychology, 30*(4), 424.
12. Baynes, K. C., Dhillo, W. S., & Bloom, S. R. (2006). Regulation of food intake by gastrointestinal hormones. *Current Opinion in Gastroenterology, 22*(6), 626–631.
13. Yamagishi, T., Horita, Y., Mifune, N., Hashimoto, H., Li, Y., Shinada, M., Miura, A., Inukai, K., Takagishi, H., & Simunovic, D. (2012). Rejection of unfair offers in the ultimatum game is no evidence of strong reciprocity. *Proceedings of the National Academy of Sciences, 109*(50), 20364-20368.
14. Pillutla, M. M., & Murnighan, J. K. (1996). Unfairness, anger, and spite: Emotional rejections of ultimatum offers. *Organizational Behavior and Human Decision Processes, 68*(3), 208-224.
15. Sanfey, A. G., Rilling, J. K., Aronson, J. A., Nystrom, L. E., Cohen, J. D. (2003). The neural basis of economic decision-making in the ultimatum game. *Science, 300*, 1755–1758.
16. Tabibnia, G., Satpute, A. B., & Lieberman, M. D. (2008). The sunny side of fairness: Preference for fairness activates reward circuitry (and disregarding unfairness activates self-control circuitry). *Psychological Science, 19*(4), 339-347.
17. Robson, S. E., Repetto, L., Gountouna, V. E., & Nicodemus, K. K. (2020). A review of neuroeconomic gameplay in psychiatric disorders. *Molecular psychiatry, 25*(1), 67-81.

18. Kaltwasser, L., Hildebrandt, A., Wilhelm, O., & Sommer, W. (2016). Behavioral and neuronal determinants of negative reciprocity in the ultimatum game. *Social Cognitive and Affective Neuroscience, 11*(10), 1608-1617.

19. Park, G. (2021). The benefit of gratitude: Trait gratitude is associated with effective economic decision-making in the ultimatum game. *Frontiers in Psychology, 12*, 590132.

20. Koo, M., Algoe, S. B., Wilson, T. D., & Gilbert, D. T. (2008). It's a wonderful life: Mentally subtracting positive events improves people's affective states, contrary to their affective forecasts. *Journal of Personality and Social Psychology, 95*(5), 1217.

21. Capra, F., Stewart, J., & Liberty Films. (1946). It's a wonderful life. Liberty Films.

22. Koo, M., Algoe, S. B., Wilson, T. D., & Gilbert, D. T. (2008). It's a wonderful life: Mentally subtracting positive events improves people's affective states, contrary to their affective forecasts. *Journal of Personality and Social Psychology,* 95(5), 1217.

23. Ang, S. H., Lim, E. A. C., Leong, S. M., & Chen, Z. (2015). In pursuit of happiness: Effects of mental subtraction and alternative comparison. *Social Indicators Research, 122*(1), 87–103.

24. Park, A., Raposo, S., & Muise, A. (2020). Does imagining you never met a romantic partner boost relationship satisfaction and gratitude? A conceptual replication and extension of the effect of mentally subtracting a partner. *Journal of Social and Personal Relationships*, 0265407520969871.

25. Pausch, R. (2008). *The last lecture.* Hachette Books.

26. Gollwitzer, P. M., & Sheeran, P. (2006). Implementation intentions and goal achievement: A meta-analysis of effects and processes. *Advances in Experimental Social Psychology, 38*, 69–119.

27. van Koningsbruggen, G. M., Stroebe, W., Papies, E. K., & Aarts, H. (2011). Implementation intentions as goal primes: Boosting self-control in tempting environments. *European Journal of Social Psychology, 41*(5), 551–557.

28. Pignatiello, G. A., Martin, R. J., & Hickman, Jr., R. L. (2020). Decision fatigue: A conceptual analysis. *Journal of Health Psychology, 25*(1), 123–135.

29. Fogg, BJ (2020). *Tiny habits: The small changes that change everything.* Houghton Mifflin Harcourt.

Chapter 4

1. Jobs, S. (2005). *Steve Jobs' commencement address on June 12, 2005.* Stanford University. Retrieved on May 27, 2021, at https://news.stanford.edu/2005/06/14/jobs-061505/

2. Snyder, C. R., Rand, K. L., & Sigmon, D. R. (2002). Hope theory: A member of the positive psychology family. In *Handbook of positive psychology,* (pp. 257–276). Oxford University Press.
3. Williams, J., & Dikes, C. (2015). The implications of demographic variables as related to burnout among a sample of special education teachers. *Education, 135*(3), 337–345.
4. Plash, S., & Piotrowski, C. (2006). Retention issues: A study of Alabama special education teachers. *Education, 127*(1), 125–128.
5. Mitchell, A., & Arnold, M. (2004). Behavior management skills as predictors of retention among South Texas special educators. *Journal of Instruction Psychology, 31*(3), 214–219.
6. Hale-Jinks, C., Knopf, H., & Kemple, K. (2006). Tackling teacher turnover in childcare: Understanding causes and consequences, identifying solutions. *Childhood Education, 82*(4), 219–226.
7. Mack, A. (2003). Inattentional blindness: Looking without seeing. *Current Directions in Psychological Science, 12*(5), 180–184.
8. Gilbert, D. (2014). *The psychology of your future self.* TED Talk.
9. Moors, A., & De Houwer, J. (2006). Automaticity: A theoretical and conceptual analysis. *Psychological Bulletin, 132*(2), 297.
10. Howell, W. S. (1982). *Conscious and competence: The empathic communicator.* University of Minnesota.
11. Getha-Taylor, H., Hummert, R., Nalbandian, J., & Silvia, C. (2013). Competency model design and assessment: Findings and future directions. *Journal of Public Affairs Education, 19*(1), 141–171.
12. Flower, J. (1999). In the mush. *Physician Executive, 25*(1), 64–66.
13. Slife, B. D. (1993). *Time and Psychological Explanation: The Spectacle of Spain's Tourist Boom and the Reinvention of Difference.* SUNY Press.
14. McDonald, H. E., & Hirt, E. R. (1997). When expectancy meets desire: Motivational effects in reconstructive memory. *Journal of Personality and Social Psychology, 72*(1), 5.
15. Patihis, L., Frenda, S. J., LePort, A. K., Petersen, N., Nichols, R. M., Stark, C. E., McGaugh, J. L., & Loftus, E. F. (2013). False memories in highly superior autobiographical memory individuals. *Proceedings of the National Academy of Sciences, 110*(52), 20947-20952.
16. Salvaggio, M. (2018). The justification of reconstructive and reproductive memory beliefs. *Philosophical Studies, 175*(3), 649-663.
17. Gilbert, D. (2014). *The psychology of your future self.* TED Talk.
18. Quoidbach, J., Gilbert, D. T., & Wilson, T. D. (2013). The end of history illusion. *Science, 339*(6115), 96-98.

19. Waitzkin, J. (2007). *The art of learning: A journey in the pursuit of excellence.* Simon and Schuster.

20. Grant, A. (2021). *Think again: The power of knowing what you don't know.* Penguin.

21. Grant, A. (2020). *Taken for granted: Daniel Kahneman doesn't trust your intuition. WorkLife with Adam Grant.* Apple Podcasts. Retrieved on May 27, 2021, at https://podcasts.apple.com/us/podcast/taken-for-granted-daniel-kahneman-doesnt-trust-your/id1346314086?i=1000513174086

22. Kahneman, D. (2011). *Thinking, fast and slow.* Macmillan.

Chapter 5

1. Holz, J., Piosczyk, H., Landmann, N., Feige, B., Spiegelhalder, K., Riemann, D., Nissen, C., & Voderholzer, U. (2012). The timing of learning before night-time sleep differentially affects declarative and procedural long-term memory consolidation in adolescents. *PLoS One, 7*(7), e40963.

2. Bunyalug, M., & Kanchanakhan, N. (2017). Effect of using smartphone before bed on sleep quality among undergraduate students at cChulalongkorn University, Thailand. *Journal of Health Research, 31*(Suppl. 2), S225-231.

3. Deloitte. (2017). *2017 Global Mobile Consumer Survey: US edition: The dawn of the next era in mobile.* Retrieved on May 28, 2021, at https://www2.deloitte.com/content/dam/Deloitte/us/Documents/technology-media-telecommunications/us-tmt-2017-global-mobile-consumer-survey-executive-summary.pdf

4. Randjelović, P., Stojiljković, N., Radulović, N., Ilić, I., Stojanović, N., & Ilić, S. (2019). The association of smartphone usage with subjective sleep quality and daytime sleepiness among medical students. *Biological Rhythm Research, 50*(6), 857-865.

5. Min, J. K., Doryab, A., Wiese, J., Amini, S., Zimmerman, J., & Hong, J. I. (2014, April). Toss'n'turn: Smartphone as sleep and sleep quality detector. In *Proceedings of the SIGCHI conference on human factors in computing systems* (pp. 477–486).

6. Bunyalug, M., & Kanchanakhan, N. (2017). Effect of using smartphone before bed on sleep quality among undergraduate students at Chulalongkorn University, Thailand. *Journal of Health Research, 31*(Suppl. 2), S225-231.

7. Zhang, M. X., & Wu, A. M. (2020). Effects of smartphone addiction on sleep quality among Chinese university students: The mediating role of self-regulation and bedtime procrastination. *Addictive Behaviors, 111,* 106552.

8. McAdams, D. P., & McLean, K. C. (2013). Narrative identity. *Current Directions in Psychological Science, 22*(3), 233–238.
9. Hardy, B. (2020). Take ownership of your future self. *Harvard Business Review.* Retrieved on May 27, 2021, at https://hbr.org/2020/08/take-ownership-of-your-future-self
10. Bodner, R., & Prelec, D. (2003). Self-signaling and diagnostic utility in everyday decision making. *The Psychology of Economic Decisions, 1*(105), 26.
11. Ferriss, T. (2019). Josh Waitzkin on how to structure your day for peak performance. *The Tim Ferriss Show. YouTube:* Tim Ferriss. Retrieved on May 27, 2021, at https://www.youtube.com/watch?v=FEOjCUkjG0k
12. Ritter, S. M., Strick, M., Bos, M. W., Van Baaren, R. B., & Dijksterhuis, A. P. (2012). Good morning creativity: Task reactivation during sleep enhances beneficial effect of sleep on creative performance. *Journal of Sleep Research, 21*(6), 643–647.
13. Shannon, B. J., Dosenbach, R. A., Su, Y., Vlassenko, A. G., Larson-Prior, L. J., Nolan, T. S., Snyder, A. Z., & Raichle, M. E. (2013). Morning-evening variation in human brain metabolism and memory circuits. *Journal of Neurophysiology, 109*(5), 1444–1456.
14. Cameron, J. (2016). *The artist's way: A spiritual path to higher creativity.* Penguin.
15. Cai, D. J., Mednick, S. A., Harrison, E. M., Kanady, J. C., & Mednick, S. C. (2009). REM, not incubation, improves creativity by priming associative networks. *Proceedings of the National Academy of Sciences, 106(*25), 10130-10134.
16. Rohn, J. (1994). *The art of exceptional living.* Nightingale-Conant/Simon & Schuster Audio.
17. Seligman, M. E., Steen, T. A., Park, N., & Peterson, C. (2005). Positive psychology progress: Empirical validation of interventions. *American Psychologist, 60*(5), 410.
18. Wood, A. M., Joseph, S., Lloyd, J., & Atkins, S. (2009). Gratitude influences sleep through the mechanism of pre-sleep cognitions. *Journal of Psychosomatic Research, 66*(1), 43–48.
19. Jackowska, M., Brown, J., Ronaldson, A., & Steptoe, A. (2016). The impact of a brief gratitude intervention on subjective well-being, biology and sleep. *Journal of Health Psychology, 21*(10), 2207–2217.
20. Sitzmann, T., & Yeo, G. (2013). A meta-analytic investigation of the within-person self-efficacy domain: Is self-efficacy a product of past performance or a driver of future performance? *Personnel Psychology, 66*(3), 531–568.
21. Fogg, BJ (2020). *Tiny habits: The small changes that change everything.* Houghton Mifflin Harcourt.

22. Koch, R. (2011). *The 80/20 principle: The secret of achieving more with less: Updated 20th anniversary edition of the productivity and business classic.* Hachette UK.
23. Koch, R. (2005). *The 80/20 individual: How to build on the 20% of what you do best.* Currency.
24. Collins, J. (2001). *Good to great: Why some companies make the leap and others don't.* HarperBusiness.
25. Sullivan, D. (2013). *How to build confidence every day.* YouTube: Strategic Coach. Retrieved on May 27, 2021, at https://www.youtube.com/watch?v=T4XWv-gP6dE&t=9s
26. Muire, Madison. (2020). Alarming habits: We surveyed 2,000 Americans to examine some of their habits when it comes to alarms and waking up in the morning. OnePoll study with Mattress Nerd. Retrieved on May 29, 2021, at https://www.mattressnerd.com/alarming-habits/
27. Fogg, BJ (2020). *Tiny habits: The small changes that change everything.* Houghton Mifflin Harcourt.
28. Fogg, B. J. (2019). *Fogg's behavior model.* Behavior Design Lab, Stanford University. Stanford, CA, USA, Tech. Rep. BehavioralModel.org
29. Ross, L., & Nisbett, R. E. (2011). *The person and the situation: Perspectives of social psychology.* Pinter & Martin Publishers.
30. Pignatiello, G. A., Martin, R. J., & Hickman, Jr., R. L. (2020). Decision fatigue: A conceptual analysis. *Journal of Health Psychology, 25*(1), 123-135.
31. Schwartz, B. (2004). *The paradox of choice: Why more is less.* New York: Ecco.
32. Johnston, W. A., & Dark, V. J. (1986). Selective attention. *Annual Review of Psychology, 37*(1), 43-75.
33. Itthipuripat, S., Cha, K., Byers, A., & Serences, J. T. (2017). Two different mechanisms support selective attention at different phases of training. *PLoS Biology, 15*(6), e2001724.
34. James, William. (1890). The principles of psychology. Classics in the History of Psychology website by C. D. Green. https://psychclassics.yorku.ca/James/Principles/
35. Ravikant, N. (2016). Naval Ravikant on happiness hacks and the 5 chimps theory (#136). *The Tim Ferriss Show.* Retrieved on March 29, 2021, at https://tim.blog/naval-ravikant-on-the-tim-ferriss-show-transcript/
36. Craig, L. (2016). *Bad timing: Balancing work and family in the 24/7 economy.* The University of New South Wales. Arts and Sciences. Retrieved on June 3, 2021, at https://www.youtube.com/watch?v=zG4bWDuhHbc

37. Cialdini, R. B., Trost, M. R., & Newsom, J. T. (1995). Preference for consistency: The development of a valid measure and the discovery of surprising behavioral implications. *Journal of Personality and Social Psychology, 69*(2), 318.

Chapter 6

1. Strauss, Valerie. (2018). Stephen Hawking famously said, "Intelligence is the ability to adapt to change." But did he really say it? *Washington Post.* Retrieved on May 30, 2021, at https://www.washingtonpost.com/news/answer-sheet/wp/2018/03/29/stephen-hawking-famously-said-intelligence-is-the-ability-to-adapt-to-change-but-did-he-really-say-it/
2. Katie, B. (2002). *Loving what is: Four questions that can change your life.* Crown Archetype.
3. Sullivan, D. (2019). *Always be the buyer: Attracting other people's highest commitment to your biggest and best standards.* The Strategic Coach Inc.
4. Bond, F. W., Hayes, S. C., & Barnes-Holmes, D. (2006). Psychological flexibility, ACT, and organizational behavior. *Journal of Organizational Behavior Management, 26*(1-2), 25-54.
5. Ciarrochi, J., Bilich, L., & Godsell, C. (2010). Psychological flexibility as a mechanism of change in acceptance and commitment therapy. In *Assessing mindfulness and acceptance processes in clients: Illuminating the theory and practice of change* (pp. 51–75). Context Press.
6. Kashdan, T. B., & Rottenberg, J. (2010). Psychological flexibility as a fundamental aspect of health. *Clinical Psychology Review, 30*(7), 865-878.
7. McCracken, L. M., & Morley, S. (2014). The psychological flexibility model: A basis for integration and progress in psychological approaches to chronic pain management. *The Journal of Pain, 15*(3), 221-234.
8. Boykin, D. M., Anyanwu, J., Calvin, K., & Orcutt, H. K. (2020). The moderating effect of psychological flexibility on event centrality in determining trauma outcomes. *Psychological Trauma: Theory, Research, Practice, and Policy, 12*(2), 193.
9. Banayan, A. (2018). *The third door: The wild quest to uncover how the world's most successful people launched their careers.* Currency.
10. Tong, E. M., Fredrickson, B. L., Chang, W., & Lim, Z. X. (2010). Re-examining hope: The roles of agency thinking and pathways thinking. *Cognition and Emotion, 24*(7), 1207–1215.
11. Snyder, C. R., LaPointe, A. B., Jeffrey Crowson, J., & Early, S. (1998). Preferences of high- and low-hope people for self-referential input. *Cognition & Emotion, 12*(6), 807–823.

12. Chang, E. C. (1998). Hope, problem-solving ability, and coping in a college student population: Some implications for theory and practice. *Journal of Clinical Psychology, 54*(7), 953–962.
13. Snyder, C. R., Shorey, H. S., Cheavens, J., Pulvers, K. M., Adams III, V. H., & Wiklund, C. (2002). Hope and academic success in college. *Journal of Educational Psychology, 94*(4), 820.
14. Law, C. & Lacey, M. Y. (2019). How entrepreneurs create high-hope environments. *Graziadio Business Report, 22*(1), 1–18.
15. Raphiphatthana, B., & Jose, P. (2021). High hope and low rumination are antecedents of grit. In *Multidisciplinary perspectives on grit: Contemporary theories, assessments, applications and critiques* (pp. 173–191). Springer International.
16. Johnson, Spencer. (2009). *Peaks and valleys: Making good and bad times work for you—at work and in life.* Atria Books.
17. Norton, R. (2013). *The power of starting something stupid: How to crush fear, make dreams happen and live without regret.* Shadow Mountain.
18. Orwell, George. (1949). *1984*. Secker & Warburg.
19. Palahniuk, C. (2000). *Invisible monsters*. Random House.
20. Sullivan, D. (2019). *Always be the buyer: Attracting other people's highest commitment to your biggest and best standards.* The Strategic Coach Inc.
21. Sill, S. (1971). *Great experiences*. The Church of Jesus Christ of Latter-Day Saints. Retrieved on June 3, 2021, at https://churchofjesuschrist.org/study/general-conference/1971/04/great-experiences
22. Janoff-Bulman, R. (1992). *Shattered assumptions: Towards a new psychology of trauma*. New York, NY: Free Press
23. Simmen-Janevska, K., Brandstätter, V., & Maercker, A. (2012). The overlooked relationship between motivational abilities and posttraumatic stress: A review. *European Journal of Psychotraumatology, 3*(1), 18560.
24. Livingston, G. (2009). *Too soon old, Too late smart: Thirty true things you need to know now.* Da Capo Lifelong Books.
25. Harmon-Jones, E., Harmon-Jones, C., & Price, T. F. (2013). What is approach motivation? *Emotion Review, 5*(3), 291-295.
26. Jang, H., and Kim, J. (2017). A meta-analysis on relationship between post-traumatic growth and related variables. *Korean Journal of Counseling. 18*, 85–105.
27. Johnson, K. J., & Fredrickson, B. L. (2005). "We all look the same to me:" Positive emotions eliminate the own-race bias in face recognition. *Psychological Science, 16*(11), 875–881.

28. Yang, S. K., & Ha, Y. (2019). Predicting posttraumatic growth among firefighters: The role of deliberate rumination and problem-focused coping. *International Journal of Environmental Research and Public Health, 16*(20), 3879.

29. Tedeschi, R. G., & Calhoun, L. G. (2004). Posttraumatic growth: Conceptual foundations and empirical evidence. *Psychological Inquiry, 15*(1), 1–18.

30. Calhoun, L. G., & Tedeschi, R. G. (2006). The foundation of posttraumatic growth: An expanded framework. In *Handbook of Posttraumatic Growth: Research and Practice* (pp. 18–64). Lawrence Erlbaum Associates.

31. Triplett, K. N., Tedeschi, R. G., Cann, A., Calhoun, L. G., & Reeve, C. L. (2012). Posttraumatic growth, meaning in life, and life satisfaction in response to trauma. *Psychological Trauma: Theory, Research, Practice, and Policy, 4*(4), 400–410.

32. American Psychological Association (2003). "Journaling": Open up! Writing about trauma reduces stress, aids immunity. American Psychological Association. Retrieved on March 2, 2021, at https://www.apa.org/research/action/writing

33. Zhou, X., & Wu, X. (2015). Longitudinal relationships between gratitude, deliberate rumination, and posttraumatic growth in adolescents following the Wenchuan earthquake in China. *Scandinavian Journal of Psychology, 56*(5), 567–572.

34. Kim, E., & Bae, S. (2019). Gratitude moderates the mediating effect of deliberate rumination on the relationship between intrusive rumination and post-traumatic growth. *Frontiers in Psychology, 10*, 2665.

35. Taleb, N. N. (2012). *Antifragile: Things that gain from disorder.* Random House Incorporated.

Conclusion

1. Sparacino, B. (2020). One day you're going to look back and realize just how far you have come. *Thought Catalog.* Retrieved June 4, 2021, at https://thoughtcatalog.com/bianca-sparacino/2016/09/one-day-youre-going-to-look-back-and-realize-just-how-far-you-have-come/

2. Sullivan, D. (2019). *Always be the buyer: Attracting other people's highest commitment to your biggest and best standards.* The Strategic Coach Inc.

REFERENCES

Al-Menayes, J. (2016). The fear of missing out scale: Validation of the Arabic version and correlation with social media addiction. International Journal of Applied Psychology, 6(2), 41-46.

Amemiya, R., & Sakairi, Y. (2019). The effects of passion and mindfulness on the intrinsic motivation of Japanese athletes. Personality and Individual Differences, 142, 132-138.

American Psychological Association. (2003). "Journaling": Open up! Writing about trauma reduces stress, aids immunity. American Psychological Association. Retrieved on March 2, 2021, at https://www.apa.org/research/action/writing

Ang, S. H., Lim, E. A. C., Leong, S. M., & Chen, Z. (2015). In pursuit of happiness: effects of mental subtraction and alternative comparison. Social Indicators Research, 122(1), 87–103.

Baer, D. (2013). How Arianna Huffington Networks without networking. Fast Company. Retrieved on June 3, 2021, at https://www.fastcompany.com/3018307/how-arianna-huffington-networks-without-networking

Banayan, A. (2018). The Third Door: The Wild Quest to Uncover How the World's Most Successful People Launched Their Careers. Currency.

Barnard, J. W. (2008). Narcissism, over-optimism, fear, anger, and depression: The interior lives of corporate leaders. University of Cincinnati Law Review, 77, 405.

Bay, C. (1970). The Structure of Freedom. Stanford University Press.

Baynes, K. C., Dhillo, W. S., & Bloom, S. R. (2006). Regulation of food intake by gastrointestinal hormones. Current Opinion in Gastroenterology, 22(6), 626–631.

Bhadra, U. (2017). The human perception, cognition, and related epigenetics. Gerontology & Geriatrics: Research, 2017; 3(1), 1030.

Bodner, R., & Prelec, D. (2003). Self-signaling and diagnostic utility in everyday decision making. The Psychology of Economic Decisions, 1(105), 26.

Bond, F. W., Hayes, S. C., & Barnes-Holmes, D. (2006). Psychological flexibility, ACT, and organizational behavior. Journal of Organizational Behavior Management, 26(1-2), 25–54.

Bonneville-Roussy, A., Lavigne, G. L., & Vallerand, R. J. (2011). When passion leads to excellence: The case of musicians. Psychology of Music, 39(1), 123–138.

Boykin, D. M., Anyanwu, J., Calvin, K., & Orcutt, H. K. (2020). The moderating effect of psychological flexibility on event centrality in determining trauma outcomes. Psychological Trauma: Theory, Research, Practice, and Policy, 12(2), 193.

Bunyalug, M., & Kanchanakhan, N. (2017). Effect of using smartphone before bed on sleep quality among undergraduate students at Chulalongkorn University, Thailand. Journal of Health Research, 31(Suppl. 2), S225–231.

Cai, D. J., Mednick, S. A., Harrison, E. M., Kanady, J. C., & Mednick, S. C. (2009). REM, not incubation, improves creativity by priming associative networks. Proceedings of the National Academy of Sciences, 106(25), 10130-10134.

Calhoun, L. G., & Tedeschi, R. G. The foundation of posttraumatic growth: An expanded framework. In Handbook of Posttraumatic Growth: Research and Practice; (pp. 18–64). Lawrence Erlbaum Associates.

Cameron, J. (2016). The Artist's Way: A Spiritual Path to Higher Creativity. Penguin.

Campbell, J. (2008). The Hero with a Thousand Faces (The collected works of Joseph Campbell). New World Library.

Capra, F., Stewart, J., & Liberty Films. (1946). It's a Wonderful Life. Liberty Films.

Carey, N. (2012). The Epigenetics Revolution: How Modern Biology is Rewriting Our Understanding of Genetics, Disease, and Inheritance. Columbia University Press.

Carpentier, J., Mageau, G. A., & Vallerand, R. J. (2012). Ruminations and flow: Why do people with a more harmonious passion experience higher well-being? Journal of Happiness Studies, 13(3), 501–518.

Chang, E. C. (1998). Hope, problem-solving ability, and coping in a college student population: Some implications for theory and practice. Journal of Clinical Psychology, 54(7), 953-962.

Cialdini, R. B., Trost, M. R., & Newsom, J. T. (1995). Preference for consistency: The development of a valid measure and the discovery of surprising behavioral implications. Journal of Personality and Social Psychology, 69(2), 318.

Ciarrochi, J., Bilich, L., & Godsell, C. (2010). Psychological flexibility as a mechanism of change in acceptance and commitment therapy. In Assessing Mindfulness and Acceptance Processes in Clients: Illuminating the Theory and Practice of Change (pp. 51–75). Context Press.

Cohen, S., Doyle, W. J., Turner, R. B., Alper, C. M., & Skoner, D. P. (2003). Emotional style and susceptibility to the common cold. Psychosomatic Medicine, 65(4), 652-657.

Collins, J. (2001). Good to Great: Why Some Companies Make the Leap and Others Don't. HarperBusiness.

Craig, L. (2016). Bad timing: Balancing work and family in the 24/7 economy. YouTube: UNSW Arts and Sciences. Retrieved on June 3, 2021, at https://www.youtube.com/watch?v=zG4bWDuhHbc

Crum, A. J., & Langer, E. J. (2007). Mind-set matters: Exercise and the placebo effect. Psychological Science, 18(2), 165–171.

Crum, A. J., Corbin, W. R., Brownell, K. D., & Salovey, P. (2011). Mind over milkshakes: Mindsets, not just nutrients, determine ghrelin response. Health Psychology, 30(4), 424.

Cubbon, L., Darga, K., Wisnesky, U. D., Dennett, L., & Guptill, C. (2020). Depression among entrepreneurs: A scoping review. Small Business Economics, 1-25.

Danner, D. D., Snowdon, D. A., & Friesen, W. V. (2001). Positive emotions in early life and longevity: Findings from the nun study. Journal of Personality and Social Psychology, 80(5), 804-813.

Deloitte. (2017). 2017 Global Mobile Consumer Survey: US edition: The dawn of the next era in mobile. Retrieved on May 28, 2021, at https://www2.deloitte.com/content/dam/Deloitte/us/Documents/technology-media-telecommunications/us-tmt-2017-global-mobile-consumer-survey-executive-summary.pdf

Duckworth, A. L., Peterson, C., Matthews, M. D., & Kelly, D. R. (2007). Grit: Perseverance and passion for long-term goals. Journal of Personality and Social Psychology, 92(6), 1087.

Elliot, A. J., & McGregor, H. A. (1999). Test anxiety and the hierarchical model of approach and avoidance achievement motivation. Journal of Personality and Social Psychology, 76(4), 628.

Epel, E. S., & Lithgow, G. J. (2014). Stress biology and aging mechanisms: Toward understanding the deep connection between adaptation to stress and longevity. Journals of Gerontology Series A: Biomedical Sciences and Medical Sciences, 69(Suppl. 1), S10–S16.

Erez, M., & Earley, P. C. (1993). Culture, Self-Identity, and Work. Oxford University Press on Demand.

Eysenck, M. W. (1994). Happiness: Facts and Myths. Psychology Press.

Ferriss, T. (2019). Josh Waitzkin on How to structure your day for peak performance. The Tim Ferriss Show. YouTube: Tim Ferriss. Retrieved on May 27, 2021, at https://www.youtube.com/watch?v=FEOjCUkjG0k

Flower, J. (1999). In the mush. Physician Executive, 25(1), 64–66.

Fogg, B. J. (2009). Creating persuasive technologies: An eight-step design process. In Proceedings of the 4th International Conference on Persuasive Technology (paper 44).

Fogg, B. J. (2019). Fogg's behavior model. Behavior Design Lab, Stanford University. Stanford, CA, USA, Tech. Rep. BehavioralModel.org

Fogg, BJ (2020). Tiny Habits: The Small Changes that Change Everything. Houghton Mifflin Harcourt.

Fredrickson, B. L. (2004). The broaden–and–build theory of positive emotions. Philosophical Transactions of the Royal Society of London Series B: Biological Sciences, 359(1449), 1367–1377.

Fromm, E. (1994). Escape from Freedom. Macmillan.

Gallup-Healthways Well-Being Index (2008). Poll: Unhappy workers take more sick days. As referenced in: Associated Press. (June 18, 2008).

Getha-Taylor, H., Hummert, R., Nalbandian, J., & Silvia, C. (2013). Competency model design and assessment: Findings and future directions. Journal of Public Affairs Education, 19(1), 141–171.

Gilbert, D. (2014). The psychology of your future self. TED Talk.

Godin, S. (2011). Linchpin: Are You Indispensable? Penguin.

Godin, S. (2012). Stop Stealing Dreams (What is School For?). Seth Godin.

Godin, S. (2012). The Icarus Deception: How High Will You Fly? Penguin.

Godin, S. (2015). Poke the Box: When was the Last Time You Did Something for the First Time? Penguin.

Gollwitzer, P. M., & Sheeran, P. (2006). Implementation intentions and goal achievement: A meta-analysis of effects and processes. Advances in Experimental Social Psychology, 38, 69–119.

Grant, A. (2020). Taken for granted: Daniel Kahneman doesn't trust your intuition. WorkLife with Adam Grant. Apple Podcasts. Retrieved on May 27, 2021, at https://podcasts.apple.com/us/podcast/taken-for-granted-daniel-kahneman-doesnt-trust-your/id1346314086?i=1000513174086

Grant, A. (2021). Think Again: The Power of Knowing What You Don't Know. Penguin.

Grover, Tim. (2021). Winning: The Unforgiving Race to Greatness (Tim Grover Winning Series). Scribner.

Hale-Jinks, C., Knopf, H., & Kemple, K. (2006). Tackling teacher turnover in childcare: Understanding causes and consequences, identifying solutions. Childhood Education, 82(4), 219–226.

Hardy, B. (2020). Take ownership of your future self. Harvard Business Review. Retrieved on May 27, 2021, at https://hbr.org/2020/08/take-ownership-of-your-future-self

Harmon-Jones, E., Harmon-Jones, C., & Price, T. F. (2013). What is approach motivation? Emotion Review, 5(3), 291–295.

Holz, J., Piosczyk, H., Landmann, N., Feige, B., Spiegelhalder, K., Riemann, D., Nissen, C., & Voderholzer, U. (2012). The timing of learning before night-time sleep differentially affects declarative and procedural long-term memory consolidation in adolescents. PLoS One, 7(7), e40963.

Howell, W. S. (1982). Conscious and Competence: The Empathic Communicator. University of Minnesota.

Itthipuripat, S., Cha, K., Byers, A., & Serences, J. T. (2017). Two different mechanisms support selective attention at different phases of training. PLoS Biology, 15(6), e2001724.

Jackowska, M., Brown, J., Ronaldson, A., & Steptoe, A. (2016). The impact of a brief gratitude intervention on subjective well-being, biology and sleep. Journal of Health Psychology, 21(10), 2207–2217.

Jackson, D. (1999). I know I'm being successful when. I Love Marketing. Retrieved on April 15, 2021, at https://ilovemarketing.com/i-know-im-being-successful-when/

James, William. (1890). The Principles of Psychology. Classics in the History of Psychology website by C. D. Green. https://psychclassics.yorku.ca/James/Principles/

Jan, M., Soomro, S., & Ahmad, N. (2017). Impact of social media on self-esteem. European Scientific Journal, 13(23), 329–341.

Jang, H., and Kim, J. (2017). A meta-analysis on relationship between post-traumatic growth and related variables. Korean Journal of Counseling. 18, 85–105.

Janoff-Bulman, R. (1992). Shattered assumptions: Towards a new psychology of trauma. New York, NY: Free Press.

Jansen, Dan. (2020). Dr. Jim Loehr on mental toughness, energy management, the power of journaling, and Olympic gold medals (#490). The Tim Ferriss Show. Retrieved March 2, 2021, at https://tim.blog/2020/12/28/jim-loehr-2/

Jefferson, Thomas. From Thomas Jefferson to John Page, 15 July 1763. Founders Archives. https://founders.archives.gov/documents/Jefferson/01-01-02-0004

Jobs, S. (2005). Steve Jobs' commencement address on June 12, 2005. Stanford University. Retrieved on May 27, 2021, at https://news.stanford.edu/2005/06/14/jobs-061505/

Johnson, K. J., & Fredrickson, B. L. (2005). "We all look the same to me": Positive emotions eliminate the own-race bias in face recognition. Psychological Science, 16(11), 875–881.

Johnson, Spencer (2009). Peaks and Valleys: Making Good and Bad Times Work for You—At Work and in Life. Atria Books.

Johnston, W. A., & Dark, V. J. (1986). Selective attention. Annual Review of Psychology, 37(1), 43–75.

Kahneman, D. (2011). Thinking, Fast and Slow. Macmillan.

Kaltwasser, L., Hildebrandt, A., Wilhelm, O., & Sommer, W. (2016). Behavioral and neuronal determinants of negative reciprocity in the ultimatum game. Social Cognitive and Affective Neuroscience, 11(10), 1608–1617.

Kashdan, T. B., & Rottenberg, J. (2010). Psychological flexibility as a fundamental aspect of health. Clinical Psychology Review, 30(7), 865–878.

Katie, B. (2002). Loving What Is: Four Questions That Can Change Your Life. Crown Archetype

Keller, J., & Bless, H. (2008). Flow and regulatory compatibility: An experimental approach to the flow model of intrinsic motivation. Personality and Social Psychology Bulletin, 34(2), 196–209.

Khumalo, T., & Plattner, I. E. (2019). The relationship between locus of control and depression: A cross-sectional survey with university students in Botswana. South African Journal of Psychiatry, 25(1), a1221.

Kim, E., & Bae, S. (2019). Gratitude Moderates the Mediating Effect of Deliberate Rumination on the Relationship Between Intrusive Rumination and Post-traumatic Growth. Frontiers in Psychology, 10, 2665.

Kim, M. H., Min, S., Ahn, J. S., An, C., & Lee, J. (2019). Association between high adolescent smartphone use and academic impairment, conflicts with family members or friends, and suicide attempts. PloS One, 14(7), e0219831.

Koch, R. (2005). The 80/20 Individual: How to Build on the 20% of What You Do Best. Currency.

Koch, R. (2011). The 80/20 Principle: The Secret of Achieving More with Less: Updated 20th anniversary edition of the productivity and business classic. Hachette UK.

Koo, M., Algoe, S. B., Wilson, T. D., & Gilbert, D. T. (2008). It's a wonderful life: mentally subtracting positive events improves people's affective states, contrary to their affective forecasts. Journal of Personality and Social Psychology, 95(5), 1217.

Law, C., & Lacey, M. Y. (2019). How entrepreneurs create high-hope environments. Graziadio Business Report, 22(1), 1–18.

Lawrence, Trevor. (2021). Stephen A.'s 1-on-1 interview with Trevor Lawrence before the 2021 NFL Draft. First Take. YouTube: ESPN channel. Retrieved on May 22, 2021, at https://www.youtube.com/watch?v=CjKBGp9Zrko&t=49s

Lawrence, Trevor. (2021). Twitter response to media about his Sports Illustrated comments. Retrieved on May 22, 2021, at https://twitter.com/Trevorlawrencee/status/1383467135410655235

Lease, S. H. (2004). Effect of locus of control, work knowledge, and mentoring on career decision-making difficulties: Testing the role of race and academic institution. Journal of Career Assessment, 12(3), 239–254.

Lin, L. Y., Sidani, J. E., Shensa, A., Radovic, A., Miller, E., Colditz, J. B., Hoffman, B. L., Giles, L. M., & Primack, B. A. (2016). Association between social media use and depression among US young adults. Depression and Anxiety, 33(4), 323–331.

Livingston, G. (2009). Too Soon Old, Too Late Smart: Thirty True Things You Need to Know Now. Da Capo Lifelong Books.

Lyubomirsky, S. (2011). Hedonic Adaptation to Positive and Negative Experiences. Oxford University Press.

Mack, A. (2003). Inattentional blindness: Looking without seeing. Current Directions in Psychological Science, 12(5), 180–184.

Maslow, A. H. (1943). A theory of human motivation. Psychological Review, 50(4), 370.

McAdams, D. P., & McLean, K. C. (2013). Narrative identity. Current Directions in Psychological Science, 22(3), 233–238.

McCoy, Sandi. (2020). How to measure success. Instagram ost. @Vsg_queendiet. Retrieved on May 24, 2021, at https://www.instagram.com/p/B-QMbNknkzu/

McCracken, L. M., & Morley, S. (2014). The psychological flexibility model: A basis for integration and progress in psychological approaches to chronic pain management. The Journal of Pain, 15(3), 221–234.

McDonald, H. E., & Hirt, E. R. (1997). When expectancy meets desire: Motivational effects in reconstructive memory. Journal of Personality and Social Psychology, 72(1), 5.

McKeown, G. (2021). Effortless: Make it Easier to Do What Matters Most. Currency.

Min, J. K., Doryab, A., Wiese, J., Amini, S., Zimmerman, J., & Hong, J. I. (2014). Toss 'n' turn: Smartphone as sleep and sleep quality detector. In Proceedings of the SIGCHI Conference on Human Factors in Computing Systems (pp. 477–486).

Mitchell, A., & Arnold, M. (2004). Behavior management skills as predictors of retention among South Texas special educators. Journal of Instruction Psychology, 31(3), 214–219.

Moors, A., & De Houwer, J. (2006). Automaticity: a theoretical and conceptual analysis. Psychological Bulletin, 132(2), 297.

Moskalev, A., Aliper, A., Smit-McBride, Z., Buzdin, A., & Zhavoronkov, A. (2014). Genetics and epigenetics of aging and longevity. Cell Cycle, 13(7), 1063-1077.

Muire, Madison. (2020). Alarming habits: We surveyed 2,000 Americans to examine some of their habits when it comes to alarms and waking up in the morning. OnePoll study with Mattress Nerd. Retrieved on May 29, 2021, at https://www.mattressnerd.com/alarming-habits/

National Science Foundation. (2020). COVID response tracking study. NORC at the University of Chicago. Retrieved on March 27, 2021, at https://www.norc.org/Research/Projects/Pages/covid-response-tracking-study.aspx

Ng, T. W. H., Sorensen, K. L., & Eby, L. T. (2006). Locus of control at work: A meta-analysis. Journal of Organizational Behavior, 27(8), 1057–1087.

Norton, R. (2013). The Power of Starting Something Stupid: How to Crush Fear, Make Dreams Happen and Live Without Regret. Shadow Mountain.

Okulicz-Kozaryn, A. (2014). "Freedom from" and "freedom to" across countries. Social Indicators Research, 118(3), 1009–1029.

Orwell, George. (1949). 1984. Secker & Warburg.

Palahniuk, C. (2000). Invisible Monsters. Random House.

Park, A., Raposo, S., & Muise, A. (2020). Does imagining you never met a romantic partner boost relationship satisfaction and gratitude? A conceptual replication and extension of the effect of mentally subtracting a partner. Journal of Social and Personal Relationships, 0265407520969871.

Park, C. L., & Helgeson, V. S. (2006). Introduction to the special section: Growth following highly stressful life events—current status and future directions. Journal of Consulting and Clinical Psychology, 74, 791–796.

Park, G. (2021). The benefit of gratitude: Trait gratitude Is associated with effective economic decision-making in the ultimatum game. Frontiers in Psychology, 12, 590132.

Patihis, L., Frenda, S. J., LePort, A. K., Petersen, N., Nichols, R. M., Stark, C. E., McGaugh, J. L. & Loftus, E. F. (2013). False memories in highly superior autobiographical memory individuals. Proceedings of the National Academy of Sciences, 110(52), 20947–20952.

Pausch, R. (2008). The Last Lecture. Hachette Books.

Pignatiello, G. A., Martin, R. J., & Hickman Jr, R. L. (2020). Decision fatigue: A conceptual analysis. Journal of Health Psychology, 25(1), 123–135.

Pillutla, M. M., & Murnighan, J. K. (1996). Unfairness, anger, and spite: Emotional rejections of ultimatum offers. Organizational Behavior and Human Decision Processes, 68(3), 208–224.

Plash, S., & Piotrowski, C. (2006). Retention issues: A study of Alabama special education teachers. Education, 127(1), 125–128.

Prociuk, T. J., Breen, L. J., & Lussier, R. J. (1976). Hopelessness, internal-external locus of control and depression. Journal of Clinical Psychology 32(2), 299–300.

Quoidbach, J., Gilbert, D. T., & Wilson, T. D. (2013). The end of history illusion. Science, 339(6115), 96–98.

Randjelović, P., Stojiljković, N., Radulović, N., Ilić, I., Stojanović, N., & Ilić, S. (2019). The association of smartphone usage with subjective sleep quality and daytime sleepiness among medical students. Biological Rhythm Research, 50(6), 857–865.

Raphiphatthana, B., & Jose, P. (2021). High hope and low rumination are antecedents of grit. In Multidisciplinary Perspectives on Grit: Contemporary Theories, Assessments, Applications and Critiques (pp. 173–191). Springer International Publishing.

Ravikant, N. (2016). Naval Ravikant on happiness hacks and the 5 chimps theory (#136). The Tim Ferriss Show. Retrieved on March 29, 2021, at https://tim.blog/naval-ravikant-on-the-tim-ferriss-show-transcript/

Rheinberg, F., & Engeser, S. (2018). Intrinsic motivation and flow. In Motivation and Action (pp. 579–622). Springer, Cham.

Ritter, S. M., Strick, M., Bos, M. W., Van Baaren, R. B., & Dijksterhuis, A. P. (2012). Good morning creativity: Task reactivation during sleep enhances beneficial effect of sleep on creative performance. Journal of Sleep Research, 21(6), 643–647.

Robinson, K. (2006). Do schools kill creativity? TED Talk.

Robinson, K., & Lee, J. R. (2011). Out of our minds. Tantor Media.

Robson, S. E., Repetto, L., Gountouna, V. E., & Nicodemus, K. K. (2020). A review of neuroeconomic gameplay in psychiatric disorders. Molecular Psychiatry, 25(1), 67–81.

Rohn, J. (1994). The Art of Exceptional Living. Nightingale-Conant/ Simon & Schuster Audio.

Rollings, Michaela. (2014). The difference between wanting someone and needing them. Thought Catalog. Retrieved on May 22, 2021, at https://thoughtcatalog.com/michaela-rollings/2014/05/the-difference-between-wanting-someone-and-needing-them/

Ross, L., & Nisbett, R. E. (2011). The Person and the Situation: Perspectives of Social Psychology. Pinter & Martin Publishers.

Rotter, J. B. (1966). Generalized expectancies for internal versus external control of reinforcement. Psychological Monographs: General and Applied, 80(1), 1–28.

Ryan, R. M., & Deci, E. L. (2019). Brick by brick: The origins, development, and future of self-determination theory. In Advances in Motivation Science (Vol. 6, pp. 111–156). Elsevier.

Salvaggio, M. (2018). The justification of reconstructive and reproductive memory beliefs. Philosophical Studies, 175(3), 649–663.

Sanfey A. G., Rilling J. K., Aronson J. A., Nystrom L. E., Cohen J. D. (2003). The neural basis of economic decision-making in the ultimatum game. Science, 300, 1755–1758.

Schwartz, B. (2004). The Paradox of Choice: Why More is Less. New York: Ecco.

Seifert, T., & Hedderson, C. (2010). Intrinsic motivation and flow in skateboarding: An ethnographic study. Journal of Happiness Studies, 11(3), 277–292.

Seligman, M. E. (2004). Authentic Happiness: Using the New Positive Psychology to Realize Your Potential for Lasting Fulfillment. Simon and Schuster.

Seligman, M. E., Steen, T. A., Park, N., & Peterson, C. (2005). Positive psychology progress: Empirical validation of interventions. American Psychologist, 60(5), 410.

Seneca, L. A. (2004). On the Shortness of Life (Vol. 1). Penguin UK.

Shannon, B. J., Dosenbach, R. A., Su, Y., Vlassenko, A. G., Larson-Prior, L. J., Nolan, T. S., Snyder, A. Z., & Raichle, M. E. (2013). Morning-evening variation in human brain metabolism and memory circuits. Journal of Neurophysiology, 109(5), 1444–1456.

Sharif, S. P. (2017). Locus of control, quality of life, anxiety, and depression among Malaysian breast cancer patients: The mediating role of uncertainty. European Journal of Oncology Nursing, 27, 28–35.

Sheldon, K. M., & Lyubomirsky, S. (2012). The challenge of staying happier: Testing the hedonic adaptation prevention model. Personality and Social Psychology Bulletin, 38(5), 670–680.

Shinn, F. S. (2012). The New Game of Life and How to Play it. Simon and Schuster.

Sideridis, G. D. (2008). The regulation of affect, anxiety, and stressful arousal from adopting mastery-avoidance goal orientations. Stress and Health: Journal of the International Society for the Investigation of Stress, 24(1), 55-69.

Sill, S. (1971). Great Experiences. The Church of Jesus Christ of Latter-Day Saints. Retrieved on June 3, 2021, at https://churchofjesuschrist.org/study/general-conference/1971/04/great-experiences

Simmen-Janevska, K., Brandstätter, V., & Maercker, A. (2012). The overlooked relationship between motivational abilities and posttraumatic stress: A review. European Journal of Psychotraumatology, 3(1), 18560.

Sitzmann, T., & Yeo, G. (2013). A meta-analytic investigation of the within-person self-efficacy domain: Is self-efficacy a product of past performance or a driver of future performance? Personnel Psychology, 66(3), 531–568.

Sivers, D. (2009). No yes. Either HELL YEAH! or no. Retrieved on June 3, 2021, at https://sive.rs/hellyeah

Slife, B. D. (1993). Time and Psychological Explanation: The Spectacle of Spain's Tourist Boom and the Reinvention of Difference. SUNY press.

Snyder, C. R., LaPointe, A. B., Jeffrey Crowson, J., & Early, S. (1998). Preferences of high- and low-hope people for self-referential input. Cognition & Emotion, 12(6), 807–823.

Snyder, C. R., Rand, K. L., & Sigmon, D. R. (2002). Hope theory: A member of the positive psychology family. Handbook of Positive Psychology (pp. 257–276). Oxford University Press.

Snyder, C. R., Shorey, H. S., Cheavens, J., Pulvers, K. M., Adams III, V. H., & Wiklund, C. (2002). Hope and academic success in college. Journal of Educational Psychology, 94(4), 820.

The Social Dilemma. (2020). The Social Dilemma. Netflix Original Documentary.

Stenseng, F., & Dalskau, L. H. (2010). Passion, self-esteem, and the role of comparative performance evaluation. Journal of Sport and Exercise Psychology, 32(6), 881-894.

St-Louis, A. C., Verner-Filion, J., Bergeron, C. M., & Vallerand, R. J. (2018). Passion and mindfulness: Accessing adaptive self-processes. The Journal of Positive Psychology, 13(2), 155-164.

Strassberg, D. S. (1973). Relationships among locus of control, anxiety, and valued-goal expectations. Journal of Consulting and Clinical Psychology, 41(2), 319.

Strategic Coach. (2019). Intentionality: Be the buyer not the seller. YouTube: Strategic Coach. Retrieved on June 1, 2021, at https://www.youtube.com/watch?v=yKXxxAyczFo&t=47s

Strauss, Valerie. (2018). Stephen Hawking famously said, "Intelligence is the ability to adapt to change." But did he really say it? Washington Post. Retrieved on May 30, 2021, at https://www.washingtonpost.com/news/answer-sheet/wp/2018/03/29/stephen-hawking-famously-said-intelligence-is-the-ability-to-adapt-to-change-but-did-he-really-say-it/

Sullivan, D. (2013). How to build confidence every day. YouTube: Strategic Coach. Retrieved on May 27, 2021, at https://www.youtube.com/watch?v=T4XWv-gP6dE&t=9s

Sullivan, D. (2015). Wanting what you want: Why getting what you want is incomparably better than getting what you need. The Strategic Coach Inc.

Sullivan, D. (2019). Always Be the Buyer: Attracting other people's highest commitment to your biggest and best standards. The Strategic Coach Inc.

Sullivan, D., & Hardy, B. (2020). Who Not How: The Formula to Achieve Bigger Goals Through Accelerating Teamwork. Hay House Business.

Sullivan, S. A., Thompson, A., Kounali, D., Lewis, G., & Zammit, S. (2017). The longitudinal association between external locus of control, social cognition and adolescent psychopathology. Social Psychiatry and Psychiatric Epidemiology, 52(6), 643–655.

Tabibnia, G., Satpute, A. B., & Lieberman, M. D. (2008). The sunny side of fairness: Preference for fairness activates reward circuitry (and disregarding unfairness activates self-control circuitry). Psychological Science, 19(4), 339–347.

Taleb, N. N. (2012). Antifragile: Things That Gain From Disorder. Random House Incorporated.

Tedeschi, R. G., & Calhoun, L. G. (2004). Posttraumatic growth: Conceptual foundations and empirical evidence. Psychological Inquiry, 15(1), 1–18.

Tong, E. M., Fredrickson, B. L., Chang, W., & Lim, Z. X. (2010). Re-examining hope: The roles of agency thinking and pathways thinking. Cognition and Emotion, 24(7), 1207–1215.

Tracy, B. (2003). Goals! How to Get Everything You Want—Faster Than You Ever Thought Possible. Berrett-Koehler Publishers.

Triplett, K. N., Tedeschi, R. G., Cann, A., Calhoun, L. G., & Reeve, C. L. (2012). Posttraumatic growth, meaning in life, and life satisfaction in response to trauma. Psychological Trauma: Theory, Research, Practice, and Policy, 4(4), 400–410.

Vallerand, R. J. (2010). On passion for life activities: The dualistic model of passion. In Advances in Experimental Social Psychology (Vol. 42, pp. 97–193). Academic Press.

Vallerand, R. J., Salvy, S. J., Mageau, G. A., Elliot, A. J., Denis, P. L., Grouzet, F. M., & Blanchard, C. (2007). On the role of passion in performance. Journal of Personality, 75(3), 505–534.

van Koningsbruggen, G. M., Stroebe, W., Papies, E. K., & Aarts, H. (2011). Implementation intentions as goal primes: Boosting self-control in tempting environments. European Journal of Social Psychology, 41(5), 551–557.

Veenhoven, R. (2000). Freedom and happiness: A comparative study in forty-four nations in the early 1990s. In Culture and Subjective Well-Being (pp. 257–288). MIT Press.

Verner-Filion, J., Schellenberg, B. J., Holding, A. C., & Koestner, R. (2020). Passion and grit in the pursuit of long-term personal goals in college students. Learning and Individual Differences, 83, 101939.

Vogel, E. A., Rose, J. P., Roberts, L. R., & Eckles, K. (2014). Social comparison, social media, and self-esteem. Psychology of Popular Media Culture, 3(4), 206.

Waitzkin, J. (2007). The Art of Learning: A Journey in the Pursuit of Excellence. Simon and Schuster.

Walsh, L. C., Boehm, J. K., & Lyubomirsky, S. (2018). Does happiness promote career success? Revisiting the evidence. Journal of Career Assessment, 26(2), 199–219.

Williams, J., & Dikes, C. (2015). The implications of demographic variables as related to burnout among a sample of special education teachers. Education, 135(3), 337–345.

Wood, A. M., Joseph, S., Lloyd, J., & Atkins, S. (2009). Gratitude influences sleep through the mechanism of pre-sleep cognitions. Journal of Psychosomatic Research, 66(1), 43–48.

Yamagishi, T., Horita, Y., Mifune, N., Hashimoto, H., Li, Y., Shinada, M., Miura, A., Inukai, K., Takagishi, H., & Simunovic, D. (2012). Rejection of unfair offers in the ultimatum game is no evidence of strong reciprocity. Proceedings of the National Academy of Sciences, 109(50), 20364–20368.

Yang, S. K., & Ha, Y. (2019). Predicting posttraumatic growth among firefighters: The role of deliberate rumination and problem-focused coping. International Journal of Environmental Research and Public Health, 16(20), 3879.

Zalta, E. N., Nodelman, U., Allen, C., & Anderson, R. L. (2005). Stanford Encyclopedia of Philosophy. Palo Alto CA: Stanford University.

Zeidner, M., & Matthews, G. (2005). Evaluation anxiety. In Handbook of Competence and Motivation, 141-163.

Zhang, M. X., & Wu, A. M. (2020). Effects of smartphone addiction on sleep quality among Chinese university students: The mediating role of self-regulation and bedtime procrastination. Addictive Behaviors, 111, 106552.

Zhao, Y., Niu, G., Hou, H., Zeng, G., Xu, L., Peng, K., & Yu, F. (2018). From growth mindset to grit in Chinese schools: The mediating roles of learning motivations. Frontiers in Psychology, 9, 2007.

Zhou, X., & Wu, X. (2015). Longitudinal relationships between gratitude, deliberate rumination, and posttraumatic growth in adolescents following the Wenchuan earthquake in China. Scandinavian Journal of Psychology, 56(5), 567-572.

Ziglar, Zig. (2015). Master Successful Personal Habits: Success Legacy Library. Gildan Media.

INDEX

H

I

J

K

L

M

N

O

T

W

Y

Z

DAN'S ACKNOWLEDGMENTS

Everything about *The GAP and The GAIN* as a fundamental thinking tool in Strategic Coach comes from thousands of hours of discussion with Babs Smith, my lifetime partner in all areas.

Our knowledgeable and wise team leaders Shannon Waller, Cathy Davis, and Julia Waller provided invaluable fine-tuning to the final manuscript.

Without the remarkable collaboration I have with Ben Hardy, Tucker Max, and Reid Tracy, the possibility of a book like this would always be an ideal, but not the deeply satisfying measurable achievement that it already is.

As with so many other great projects over the past two decades, I'm thankful for the entrepreneurial insights of Joe Polish and Dean Jackson.

And this book wouldn't be what it is without the many "GAP and GAIN" stories that were generously shared with us.

Thank you to the following Strategic Coach entrepreneurs who took the time to sit down for interviews with Ben and Strategic Coach team members in order to tell us about their experience of using *The GAP and The GAIN* in their own lives and businesses: Mary Atwood, Katie Baxter, Bill Bloom, Justin Breen, Andre Brisson, Claire Burroughs, Chris Carlson, Julia Carlson, Giselle Chapman, Kate Dewhirst, Howard Getson, Jamie Gutierrez, Ingrid Hibbard, Dean Jackson, Scott Jared,

Bill Keen, Pete Kofod, Beth Kraszewski, Brian Kurtz, Anna Larson, Neha Malde, Jeffrey Marks, Carolyn Nolan, Maurice Patane, Jiska Pesch-Kuilman, Katie Ridland, Eric Roman, Cheryl Sady, Chad Willardson, and Jill Young.

I'm also very grateful to our associate coaches, Russell Schmidt, Adrienne Duffy, Gary Mottershead, Gina Pellegrini, Teresa Easler, Lee Brower, Kim Butler, Mary Miller, Patti Mara, Colleen Bowler, David Batchelor, Peter Buckle, Gary Klaben, Chad Johnson, Steven Neuner, and David Braithwaite, for sharing their stories with us and for imparting *The GAP and The GAIN* concept, along with their own experience, insights, and wisdom, to thousands of Strategic Coach entrepreneurs over the years.

This mindset has benefited so many people, and it couldn't have had the reach and impact it's had without their skilled coaching.

BEN'S ACKNOWLEDGMENTS

I've been in love with *The GAP and The GAIN* concept from the first time I heard it.

It is an honor to write this book with Dan Sullivan.

I'll start by acknowledging and thanking Dan for the life-changing ideas and frameworks he comes up with. I'm just one of countless thousands whose lives have been transformed by Dan's thinking. I'd also like to thank Babs Smith for trusting me, and for allowing me to take such an intimate and unique role in the work Dan and Babs do at Strategic Coach. I know that the work being done at Strategic Coach is deeply inspired and special. I'm incredibly humbled to learn from and be a part of this important work.

Thank you to Tucker Max, for once again making this book a reality. You helped us get the book deal established with Hay House. You helped me think through the ideas of this book. You also acted as the best psychologist I've ever had, helping me get over my own emotional hurdles and baggage. Thank you for being such a clearheaded and caring person. Thank you for helping me through my emotional blocks. Thank you for helping me take ownership of my life. Thanks for helping me improve as a writer and thinker.

Thank you to the team at Hay House—Reid Tracey, Patty Gift, and Melody Guy—for choosing to work with Dan and me. It's been an absolute pleasure working with Hay House.

I've felt incredible respect and support from Reid and Patty in every interaction I've had. I've also loved working directly with Melody. She's been amazing to work with. During early stages of writing *The Gap and The Gain*, I was struggling to build the right framework for the book. In one conversation with Melody, I was able to clarify how I wanted this book to flow. Thank you to all of you!

Thank you to my mom, Susan Knight, for spending several multi-hour sessions going through this book with me. We hop on Zoom together and she allows me to read the hideous and disjointed drafts of my books *OUT LOUD* to her. She has incredible intuition and care as we work slowly through every word and sentence together. Mom, thank you so much for your constant love and support for me and my work. These books wouldn't be nearly as good without you.

To my beautiful wife, Lauren, and to our six amazing kids—Kaleb, Jordan, Logan, Zorah, Phoebe, and Rex. Lauren, thank you for encouraging and supporting me on my good days and especially on my bad ones. Thanks for always trusting in me and helping me believe I can continue to grow and succeed as a person, as a man, as a husband, and as a father. To my kids: Thank you all for being in my life. Thank you for being such a huge inspiration and support to me. You make me better every day. I've learned more about *The GAP and The GAIN* through you than through anyone else. I commit to being in the GAIN more and more for you in the future, so I can help you realize just how amazing you truly are.

To my dad, Philip Hardy, thank you for being a remarkable dad. Thank you for transforming your own challenges and hardships into GAINS in your own life. Thank you for being an example of someone who is continuing to grow and progress, regardless of what happened in the past. You're amazing! Thanks for being a huge supporter of me and my family. Thank you to my brothers, Trevor and Jacob. You are both so important to me. I love you both very much.

Finally, to God. Thank you for giving me this life. It is a truly incredible education and experience. Thank you for the opportunity and ability to transform all of my experiences into GAINS. Thank you for all the wisdom, learning, and intelligence you generously shower upon me. Thank you for seeing my GAINS and not my GAPS. I feel close to you. I know I'm loved. I know you are helping me continue to grow in my GAINS. Thank you.

ABOUT THE AUTHORS

Dan Sullivan is the world's foremost expert on entrepreneurship and has coached more successful entrepreneurs than anyone on the planet. He is the cofounder of Strategic Coach®, the leading entrepreneurial coaching program in the world, and author of more than 50 publications on entrepreneurial success. Over the past 30-plus years, Strategic Coach has provided teaching and training to more than 20,000 entrepreneurs.

www.strategiccoach.com

Dr. Benjamin Hardy is an organizational psychologist and author of *Willpower Doesn't Work* and *Personality Isn't Permanent.* Together, he and Dan co-authored the national bestseller *Who Not How* and *The Gap and The Gain.* His blogs have been read by more than 100 million people and are featured in the *Harvard Business Review, The New York Times, Forbes, Fortune,* CNBC, and others. For several years, he was the #1 most-read writer on Medium.com. He and his wife, Lauren, are the parents of six kids. They live in Orlando, Florida.

www.benjaminhardy.com

WRITE DOWN YOUR GAINS

WRITE DOWN YOUR GAINS

WRITE DOWN YOUR GAINS

WRITE DOWN YOUR GAINS

WRITE DOWN YOUR GAINS

WRITE DOWN YOUR GAINS

We hope you enjoyed this Hay House book. If you'd like to receive our online catalog featuring additional information on Hay House books and products, or if you'd like to find out more about the Hay Foundation, please contact:

Hay House, Inc., P.O. Box 5100, Carlsbad, CA 92018-5100
(760) 431-7695 or (800) 654-5126
(760) 431-6948 (fax) or (800) 650-5115 (fax)
www.hayhouse.com® • www.hayfoundation.org

Published in Australia by: Hay House Australia Pty. Ltd.,
18/36 Ralph St., Alexandria NSW 2015
Phone: 612-9669-4299 • *Fax:* 612-9669-4144
www.hayhouse.com.au

Published in the United Kingdom by: Hay House UK, Ltd.,
The Sixth Floor, Watson House, 54 Baker Street, London W1U 7BU
Phone: +44 (0)20 3927 7290 • *Fax:* +44 (0)20 3927 7291
www.hayhouse.co.uk

Published in India by: Hay House Publishers India,
Muskaan Complex, Plot No. 3, B-2, Vasant Kunj, New Delhi 110 070
Phone: 91-11-4176-1620 • *Fax:* 91-11-4176-1630
www.hayhouse.co.in
